TRUE
TALES
of
WESTERN
CANADA

VOLUME THREE

Gopher Book No. 12

DEDICATED TO

Terry Miller

Published by:

Frank W. Anderson,
P.O. Box 9055,
Saskatoon, Sask.,
S7K 7E7

TABLE OF CONTENTS

Sagas Of The West appears about three times a year

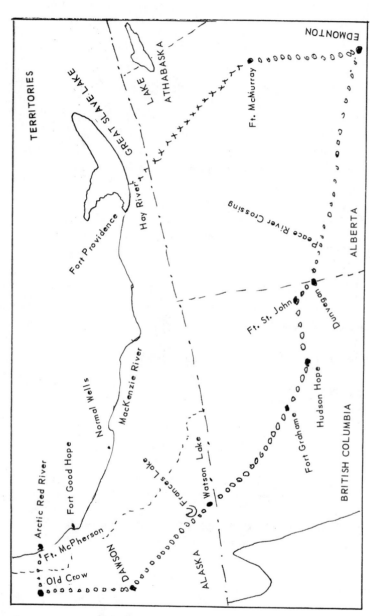

4

The Klondyke Trail from Edmonton

by HAROLD FRYER

Twenty some odd miles west of the thriving Peace River country city of Grande Prairie stand the boarded up remains of an old single-room school. Called the Klondike Trail school, it sits directly on one of the many trails followed by the gold seekers who headed overland from Edmonton to seek their fortunes in the famous gold camps of the Yukon. Who were these intrepid men, where did they hail from and why did they choose an overland route to the Klondike when the sea route up the west coast of British Columbia and across the Chilkoot Pass was obviously much easier?

To the first question, it need only be said that they were ordinary men (and women) like you and me - - mostly young folks with a strong spark of adventure in their souls. Gold Hungry? Probably no more so than we. Suffice it to say that they were willing to take a few risks in the hope of striking it rich.

Where did they come from? From the British Iles, from Australia and South Africa - but mostly from Canada and the United States.

Why did they choose the Edmonton Route? Some say they were lured that way by unscrupulous businessmen anxious to make a fast buck. Historians like James MacGregor disagree. What seems to have happened was that the potential gold seekers simply got out a map of North America, discovered Edmonton was the closest point to the Klondike that could be reached by railroad and chose it as their starting place.

Actually, it was only after the Edmonton town council, Board of Trade and the **Edmonton Journal** began getting inquiries from prospective gold seekers that the **Bulletin** began promoting Edmonton as the logical jumping-off spot to the Klondike. Enterprising merchants took it from there and began stocking every conceivable item that a man would need on a hike that could take more than a year to accomplish. Once hit with the bug, the **Bulletin** editor and the Board of Trade probably did try to over-sell the "All Canadian" Route, but it was the gold seekers themselves who initiated the route and the onus was therefore on their shoulders to get through, turn back or die in the attempt.

Regardless of how they fared enroute, the Klondkiers followed basically two approaches from Edmonton - the overland route and the water route. Those taking the water route went overland to Athabasca Landing or Peace River Crossing where they built boats and floated down these rivers to the Mackenzie River and down the Mackenzie to the mouth of either the Peel or the Rat Rivers in the Mackenzie Delta. From there they went up either river, crossed over the Richardson Mountains till they hit the headwaters of one of the tributaries of the Yukon River - the Porcupine, for instance - floated down the tributary to the Yukon River, where they would catch a riverboat coming upriver which would take them to Dawson City and the goldfields. There were alternatives to this route, such as up the Laird River to its headwaters, overland to Frances Lake, then down the Pelly and Yukon Rivers to the Klondike. None of these approaches was easy and many died of scurvy or starvation before they got to the Klondike, if they got there at all. But all were infinitely easier than the overland path.

Actually, everyone heading for the Klondike had to start out overland initially. Although a handful of early birds got started during the summer and fall of 1897, by far the largest numbers left during the winter of 1897-98 and the following spring. Consequently, during the winter, camps

Klondikers Starting Out from Edmonton - Store in Background
Is Hudson's Bay Company

sprang up all over Edmonton, which boasted a population of 1,700. It was a boom of unprecedented proportions and all the bars, cafes, hotel and merchantile establishments did a rip-snorting business as Klondikers prepared for the long journey north.

Perhaps nowhere did the gold seekers show more inventiveness than in their means of transportation. Some chose pack horses; others dog teams; still others horse-or-ox drawn sleighs, wagons or Red River carts. But Charles Smith, of Houston, showed the most imagination of all when he started out from Edmonton with a horse-drawn conveyance that utelized whiskey barrels for wheels. Since he would have to cross many streams along the way, he naturally assumed that the whiskey barrels would float his wagon and be more practical than wheels. That his 'wheels' disintegrated four miles out is no condemnation of his ingenuity.

If the All-Canadian route began as one trail out of Edmonton, it did not remain that way long. Most trails came back together near what is now Watson Lake, Yukon, but in between St. Albert and there they fanned out and criss-crossed like rabbit tracks in the snow. Interestingly, a trail axed out by Inspector J.D. Moodie of the North West Mounted Police, leading northwest from Fort St. John, B.C., and following the Rocky Mountain Trench, was used by no more than 150 people.

The Chalmer's Trail from Edmonton to Peace River Crossing, and later known as the Klondike Trail, however, was used extensively. In the summer of 1897 when the government of what was then known as the North West Territories realized the rush to the Klondike was real, they decided to open a road. They hired a well-known guide, Dan Noyes, to look after the packing, and engineer T.W. Chalmers to map out the trail. On Sept. 9. they set out with ten horses pulling five two-wheeled carts.

According to Chalmer's report, they followed an already fair road to Lac La Nonne, some 40 miles west. It was clearly marked but in need of some repair to the Athabaska River. They crossed the river in fabric boats, but once

8

across, since the trail petered out, they were forced to abandon their carts and go on horseback with pack horses carrying their supplies.

With the six axemen Chalmers began clearing a road to Fort Assiniboine. From there he went on to Lesser Slave Lake and thence to Peace River Crossing. Long before he could finish, however, the first groups of Klondike-bound miners passed him. Meanwhile, the government was making it somewhat easier for the travellers by installing ferries on the Pembina and Athabaska Rivers, across the narrows on Lesser Slave Lake and eventually on the Peace at the crossing.

Until Chalmers cut his trail and the government installed the ferries, that first 320 miles to the Peace River Crossing was hell on horses and men and caused some 100 gold seekers to turn back. Perhaps the best way to describe some of the hardships is to refer to the diary of one who experienced it - Frank Walter, of Fort Saskatchewan - who led a party consisting of his brother, Albert W. Hepburn, John Reid and several others. He set out on March 8, 1898.

He wrote: "By the time we reached the Athabaska River, several of the parties who had gone on ahead had become very disgruntled with the route and stated so in no uncertain terms uipon blazed trees . . .

"The Hillside (north bank of the Athabaska) was littered with broken boxes, smashed sleighs and harness and practically every tree on the lower slope of the grade was blazed where owners gave vent to their feelings in epithets upon the trees . . .

"Passing along the south shore of Lesser Slave Lake we commenced to find dead horses in abundance, the majority of course dying for lack of feed . . ."

An estimated 4,000 horses died along this route, mostly due to the ignorance of the gold seekers, many of whom had no idea of the requirements of the poor beasts, but for those who realized the hazards, much of the trouble was surmounted. For instance, Dr. H.L. McInnis, of

Edmonton, set out March 24, 1898, but rather than following the Chalmer's Trail, headed for Athabasca Landing. With two men and 22 horses pulling sleighs loaded with hay, he easily got through to Lesser Slave Lake. There he bought more hay from the Hudson's Bay post and continued on to Peace River Crossing, where he arrived on April 11 with his horses fat and healthy.

If for the ignorant the trail to Peace River Crossing was hard on man and beast, none of the trails leading from there to the Klondike were all that easy. From the Crossing there was a well-used wagon road leading to Dunvegan, but from there most of the trails were nebulous. As the article title indicates, at least a few of the Klondikers crossed the Peace River at Dunvegan and headed across the great prairie on the south side of the river, eventually arriving in Fort. St. John. Most, however, stayed on the north side of the river, keeping well away from its banks. Still others, perhaps 200, followed a trail blazed by Mr. W.P. Taylor, who took a more easterly route from the Crossing, heading directly towards Fort Nelson. Joe McDonald, a well-known frontiersman, guided the C.P. Braithwaite party from Edmonton to Fort St. John. When he arrived there, he had a falling out with his employer and returned to Edmonton. Here is what he told the **Edmonton Bulletin** about part of the trip:

"From the Crossing to Dunvegan is a well beaten trail, but to follow it into Dunvegan is to make an unnecessary detour of about 30 miles in and back. By following the trail halfway to Dunvegan, at a place called Old Woman's Lake, a fairly well beaten trail made lately by travellers leads in a westerly direction. By travelling on this trail from six to eight miles and about a mile beyond Island Lake, a big trail cut out like a surveyor's line can be seen due north. By taking notice they will see a trail just there running to the left which they will follow and just on top of a little hill as they pass through some poplar they will see "OK" marked in pencil on a blazed tree. This is the trail to follow to St. John . . ."

A Boat Building Camp on the Athabaska River

For those going by way of Fort St. John, at least 300 or more, it pretty much depended what they had in mind what route they took from there. For some, getting to the Klondike was of only secondary importance. They hoped to strike it rich on the way and panned every stream as they went along. Quite a number reached Fort St. John in the fall of 1897 and many more during that winter. There and on Bear Flats, 12 miles farther up the Peace, they found plenty of feed for their horses.

The following spring many started up the Halfway River, followed it on to its headwarters, crossed over the Laurier Pass to Fort Grahame on the Finlay River. They continued up the Finlay to the mouth of the Fox River, followed it to its headwarters, crossed over the Sifton Pass and went along the Kechika River to its confluence with the Laird and followed the Laird to Lower Post near the B.C.-Yukon border. From there most struck northwest till they hit the Pelly River, where they built boats or rafts and floated down the Pelly to the Yukon River at Fort Selkirk. Then they floated down the Yukon to Dawson and the goldfields. (This was basically the route blazed by Inspector Moodie, unfortunately finished too late in 1898 to benefit many of the Klondikers.)

Not all followed this same route and not all leaving Fort St. John went that far. Maybe half turned back and some, after reaching Fort Grahame, travelled up the Finlay only as far as the mouth of the Inginaca River, then followed the Inginaca westward to the Omineca gold fields and sought their fortune there.

It all seems too easy to follow these routes on a map but little of the going was easy. Cold and scurvy faced the travellers in the winter or starvation for both man and beast. In the summer, relentlessly swarming mosquitoes tortured them night and day. Nor were these the only enemies. Most of the gold seekers were Americans with a low regard for the rights of the Indians. The grasslands near Fort St. John, on Bear Flats and along the lower reaches of the Halfway River were traditional grazing grounds for

Beaver Indian ponies. Consequently, when the Klondikers moved in their horses without asking permission, the Beavers were angry. Then when one group of Americans shot five of the Beaver Indians' prize stallions and destroyed several of their laborously constructed log bear traps when their horses blundered into them, the Beavers were enraged. Barney Maurice, a High Prairie merchant who was in Fort St. John, told how the Indians sought revenge.

"On the hill at Fort St. John, there were," he said, "about 75 buggies, wagons and Red River carts left by the miners. About 250 Indians put the whole works down the hill and I could see afterwards broken wagons and equipment for about 600 feet down. All the white men, with the exception of the doctor, myself and my partner, left at night. We had to stay, but the Indians didn't do us any harm"

Although none of the land routes were good, prehaps the best was the one blazed by W.P. Taylor, who was hired by the Edmonton town council. He set cut from Edmonton in February, 1898, mushing a team of seven dogs. He followed the Chalmer's Trail as far as it went at the time - Deer Mountain in the Swan Hills - and arrived at the H.B.C. post on Lesser Slave Lake in a week. There he hired an Indian guide and got Harry Garbutt, an adventuresome Englishman, to accompany him. Together, they reached Peace River Crossing on March 17.

From the Crossing they headed northwest towards the then deserted post of Fort Nelson, some 260 miles away. Along the way they passed Cardinal Lake, the headwaters of the White Mud and Notikewan Rivers, and crossed the upper Chinchaga River on march 15. When the snow began melting as they neared the Fontas River, Taylor unloaded the toboggans, packed his supplies on his dogs and carried on. He followed the Fontas to the Sikanni Chief River, then struck off over high ground until he intersected an Indian trail which led him to Fort Nelson. He arrived there on April 8.

13

14   A Relatively Well-to-do Boat Party on Athabaska

From Fort Nelson, Taylor followed the Muskwa River some 50 miles. turned north over a divide until he hit the Toad River, then followed it for 20 miles to its junction with the Laird at Toad River post. He crossed the Laird some four miles downstream at the mouth of the Grayling River and there left Garbett and his Indian guide to hunt while he and a guide he hired from an Indian band camped there pressed on. They travelled up the Grayling, crossed over to the headwaters of the Crow, followed it till it joined the Beaver. In turn, they crossed the Rock, Coal and Hyland Rivers and reached Frances Lake on May 19. Taylor then pressed on west till he reached the Pelly River, built a raft and floated downstream some 50 miles. Seeing traces along the bank that at least one party of Klondikers had passed that way and knowing the Pelly flowed into the Yukon River and that the rest of the journey would be a simple matter of floating downstream to Dawson City, he turned back on May 21 and headed for home.

Coming home, instead of heading for Peace River Crossing from Fort Nelson, he travelled to Fort St. John. This he claimed made for somewhat easier going than the other route. At St. John, he made a raft and floated down the Peace to Peace River Crossing, where he arrived on July 15. From there it took him only eight days to reach his home at Lac St. Anne, 35 miles west of Edmonton, and he arrived with six of his original seven dogs alive and healthy.

Altogether, Taylor travelled some 2,200 miles in 157 days, or about 14 miles a day. Of course, none of the 200 or so men who followed him could expect to make such good time for they were loaded down with nearly a ton of supplies each. However, Taylor . proved that by travelling light, the trip could be made in less than four months, rather than the year it took those lucky enough to get through. Interestingly, included in those taking the Taylor Trail was a group of Americans called the Geddis-

Harris party who were driving a herd of 50 steers. None of the steers reached the Klondike, nor did any of at least two other herds driven up the Moodie route.

"The White Pass and Yukon Railway, heading from Skagway, Alaska, to Lake Bennet, some 50 miles away, wrung the neck of Edmonton's All Canadian routes to the Yukon," wrote James MacGregor in his book **Klondike Rush Through Edmonton.** He is right, for when the gold seekers could make a leirurely boat trip up the west coast from Vancouver or Seattle to Skagway and then take the train over the White Pass to Lake Bennet where they could build a boat or raft and float down the Yukon River to Dawson City, there seemed little need to break their backs hiking the All-Canadian route.

Still, till the railroad was built in 1898, some 1,560 people, including at least 20 women and 4 children, started over the Klondike Trail from Edmonton. Of these, approximately 775 took the overland route and 785 the water route. Approximately 160 reached the Klondike by land and 565 by the river passage. Suprisingly, though the land trail was the tougher of the two, an equal number - 35 - died on each of the two routes. Sadly, the deaths included at least two babies, one of whom was conceived and born along the way.

From records we know about how many men started from Edmonton; we know what routes they took, how many died and approximately how many got through. But, how many of those who reached the Klondike struck it rich?

That is something the records do not seem to show.

Riverboat Days In Manitoba

There were two standard routes for visitors or settlers to reach Winnipeg in the 1870s. One was over the treacherous Dawson Route, partly by boat and partly by stage coach. The service was terrible; the accomodation worse; and no one who ever made the trip once repeated the experience from other than sheer necessity!

The second method to reach Manitoba from the east was to travel as far as possible by rail through the United States and then make connections via boat or stage along the Red River route. Passengers coming from the west faced a 3,000 mile trek from Vancouver up through the interior of British Columbia and along the Yellowhead route to Edmonton and thence over the old Carlton Trail to Winnipeg. Here there were neither boats nor stage coaches to ease the journey, unless one wished to take the North Saskatchewan River route through Lake Winnipeg.

The heydey of the steamboats which plied the Red River from Fisher's Landing, near Fargo, N.D., to Winnipeg, lasted from 1859 to approximately 1881. The most fascinating era was the period between 1874 and 1879.

The first vessel to make the trip was the **Anson Northup** a rickety stern-wheeler that arrived at Fort Garry on May 18, 1859 to the consternation of the Indians and the delight of the settlers. She ran successfully until the spring of 1862 when she was sunk by an ice gorge just below Fort Garry.

17

The Ansun Northup

She was replaced by the **International** that year, and this boat continued to bring supplies - and the odd passenger - to the settlement on the edge of the Great Plains.

Following the creation of Manitoba as a province in 1870, an upsurge of settlers and commerce invited the expansion of river traffic and in quick succession **The Selkirk, Dacotah, the Alpha and The Cheyenne** were built and put into operation.

Originally, these boats ran from Fargo, but with the extension of the St. Paul and Pacific railway to the banks of the Red River in 1874 a small community known as Fisher's Landing grew up around the railway station near the banks of the Red River.

The town, if such it could be called, was named after E.H. Fisher, local superintendent of the railroad. He seemed to spend most of his working day dealing with delegations of irate citizens from Winnipeg and Fargo in assuring them that the town would be 'cleaned up.'

Fisher's Landing, hazard for the early traveller to and from Manitoba, consisted mostly of saloons and boxcars on sidings. One hotel, operated by a Captain Russell, was said to be "respectable", but even it contained a club - The Honkey Tonky - which advertised whiskey and women -both apparently bad.

With the arrival of the railroad at Fisher's Landing, the river boats shifted their terminal to that point. Not to be outdone, the stage coach line of Carpenter and Blakely, which had been making bi-weekly trips to Winnipeg since 1871, also moved its southern terminus from Fargo to the Landing. So, Fisher's Landing became the transportation hub for Manitoba.

The following year, 1875, due to increased freight and passenger traffic into Manitoba, two more steamers were added to the paddlewheel fleet - **The Manitoba** and the **Minnesota. The Manitoba**, a famous boat on the prairies, was built in Fargo that year, saw service on the Winnipeg run until 1882, when she was moved to the North Saskatchewan River. She was wrecked near Prince Albert in 1885.

The rise of Fisher's Landing broung an old and dishonorable sprofession to the doorstep of Manitoba - the river boat gambler. The first of these to take up residence at the Landing was Charles Stanton - better known by his tradename 'Shang'. He was followed shortly by Oscar L. Rose, otherwise glorying in the soft-sell title of Farmer Brown.

Shang, every bit the dandy, worked the trains from the east as well as frequenting the many saloons at the Landing. Occasionally he took a jaunt down the river to Winnipeg, but since gambling was discouraged by the river captains, these trips were more in the nature of pleasure excursions. When business was dull during the ice-bound winter months, he wandered off to the Black Hills for more trade. His forte was 3 card Monte.

Farmer Brown, on the other hand, affected a picture of benign friendliness. A reporter who met him in 1877 wrote: "His place of abode is a saloon near the steamboat warf and his family consists of several adult females. He is about 30 years of age and of fair complexion.

19

"He has an expression of countenance which is eminently kindly. He was attired in the ordinary garb of the pioneer, without either coat or waistcoat, with his shirt wide open at the neck in front, and with a broad straw hat carelessly flung upon the back of his head."

Though he may have appeared kindly, Oscar "Farmer Brown" Rose was as deadly as the rest. In the summer of 1876, two young soldiers from the Winnipeg barracks were at the Landing while awaiting train connections to the east. They became involved in a 3 card Monte game at Brown's but felt that they were being cheated and objected. One, Parks, had his head split open in three places. The following morning, his companion, being unable to find him, had to catch their train after turning over the matter to the Fargo police. It was suspected that he had met with foul play, but nothing could be proven.

A year later, Farmer Brown was sentenced to five years in the Michigan State Penitentiary for a series of offences.

Other notorious gamblers who preyed upon the credulous and the unwary were Norwegin Jim, Bob Shaw and Pete Brannigan. A distinct aid to the success of their operations was that their victims were travelling and any kind of delay in their journey could be expensive. Few of the fleeced sheep could afford to spend the necessary time for a successful prosecution.

From Fisher's Landing, the immigrant bound for the delights of Winnipeg and the Great North West could embark upon one of the several river boats or take passage by stage. The stage fare was $12 in summer, $24 in winter, with no competition.

There were only a few settlements along the Red River. The first was Georgetown, 15 miles north of Fisher's Landing; then Goose River, Frog Point and Grand Forks. Between Grand Forks and Winnipeg - a distance of nearly 200 miles by water - the only notable settlements were Pembina and Emerson.

A suprising number of passengers were "drowned", to use the phrase of that day. The word covered all sorts of

21

WINNIPEG, ET FORT-GARRY À GAUCHE, ARRIVÉE DES MENNONITES.

WINNIPEG, SUR LA RIVIÈRE ROUGE.

Winnipeg from St. Boniface, 1874 (top left); The Immigration Shed (top right)
Main Street, Winnipeg (lower)

mysterious disappearances from shipboard. Undoubtedly, many were knocked unconscious, robbed and thrown over the rails.

At Winnipeg, if friends were not waiting, the landed immigrant could be housed free of charge at the Immigrant Shed which stood on the bank of the Red River, near its junction with the Assiniboine, or take rooms in one of the many hotels along Main Street.

The arrival of a boatload of Easterners was the signal for a particularily obnoxious brand of sneak thief to appear at the Shed. One of their favorite tracks was to mingle with the newly arrived passengers - sometimes there would be as many as 300 passengers on the same boat - and find out where they kept their valuables. When their selected victim bedded down for the night on the wooden floor, the thieves 'slept' beside them. In the night, the thieves and possessions departed.

Strangely, the Winnipeg of this period was not plagued with gamblers. The main hazards to the traveller were the confidence men, the phoney real estate dealers and the 'waitresses' who infested the hotels and restaurants. Frequently, the newcomer's sleep was disturbed by boisterous lads shooting off their revolvers in the middle of the night or by some enterprising character trying to sell them an Indian girl slave for $3.00, but for the most part the perils were over once the haven of the plains was reached.

From Winnipeg, the traveller could go north to Selkirk either by one of the smaller river boats, such as the **Swallow** or **Kewatin**, or take one of the stages. The **Prince Rupert** was the principal boat on the Assiniboine River west to Portage la Prairie, but stiff competition was given by a coach line operated by John McKenney.

Anyone foolish, or unwary enough, to want to go east to the Lake of the Woods district either walked or hazarded their life and limbs to the uncertain - and infrequent service - of the stages that dared the rugged roads east.

There was a distinctly different atmosphere on the river boats that ran north and west from Winnipeg. For the most part, the skippers and crews were family men who tolerated no gamblers, kept the fancy ladies under wraps, and transported their cargoes with a remarkable degree of safety. Seldom was a passenger 'lost overboard' in contrast to the mysterious disappearances from the big boats.

Nevertheless, there was plenty of excitement. River boat captains were a proud lot and seldom passed up the opportunity for a race. The Red River presented sufficient hazards in its sand banks, swift currents and fog patches to satisfy the most adventuresome crew, but when to these was added the spectacle of two churning paddle-wheelers charging down the middle of the stream, collisions were inevitable. Some of the boats seemed to spend as much time on the bottom as on the top.

Another danger to early travellers was the use of the rivers by the stage lines in winter. Since the rivers were more solid in winter than the roads, the drivers tended to test them out early at freeze-up and to stay on them as long as possible in the spring. This practice led to numerous incidents when the stage, horses and passengers went though the rotten ice.

The colorful era did not last long, however, for by 1879 trains were running south, north and east from Winnipeg. Fittingly, the first locomotive was brought in by river barge. Within two more years, west-bound trains made their appearance and - except in the remoter areas - the river boat and stage coach followed each other into oblivion.

Lynch Justice
In British Columbia

Justice, like life itself on the British Columbia frontier, could be a somewhat rough-and-tumble affair, calling more for commonsense and an individualistic approach, perhaps, than for the finer points of British jurisprudence. Yet, for all of its homespun flavor, the mills of justice did grind finely. Dedicated officers of a tiny provincial police force guarded the peace throughout a province greater in size and more formidable in geography than most European nations. Under the direction of such austere figures as Chief Justice Matthew Begbie, the mismaned "Hanging Judge", these men laid the foundation for law and order, ensuring in the process that the chaotic conditions which ruled south of the 49th parallel did not become part and parcel of pioneer life in B.C.

However, despite having been virtually ignored by historians, British Columbia has in fact known the grim presence of Judge Lynch - - not once but three times.! By far the most controversial incident involving vigilante action, which created nothing less than an international furore and resounded as far as Ottawa and Washington, D.C., was the hanging of a young Sumas Indian brave by Americans in 1884.

Today, almost a century after, the tragic case of Loui Sam retains all of the drama and tragedy which had *. entire Pacific Northwest embroiled in argument . . .

When first word of the incident was flashed throug¹ the province by telegraph, tempers flared - an outriged **Victoria Colonist** paper expressing the province's anger in a searing editorial: "The news that . . . a large number of settlers from the American side had crossed the border,

by T. W. Paterson   25

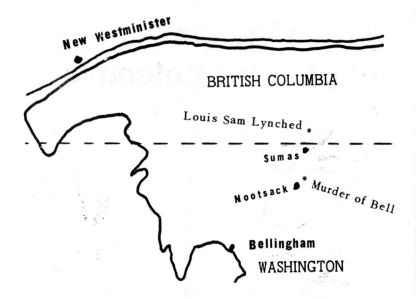

taken the Indian who was suspected of murdering a Mr. Bell, living near Nootsack, from British custody and summarily hanged him, should excite as great a thrill of horror as the murder they sought to avenge by perpetrating the same crime themselves . . .''

The story behind this forgotten 'cas celebre' had begun two nights before at Sumas, B.C., when Washington Territory resident, Robert C. Breckenridge, had breathlessly called at the office of William M. Campbell, Justice of the Peace, to inform him that Nootsack Crossing merchant, James Bell, had been murdered, the evidence pointing to a Canadian Indian named Louis Sam.

Mr. Campbell immediately went into action. Naming settlers Thomas York and J.C. Steele as his special constables, he sought out the wanted man, who surrendered without a struggle. This accomplished, Campbell ordered his deputies to escort Sam to New Westminster.

Unfortunately for Sam - as events were to prove - it was late and the Royal City at the end of a long journey factors which prompted his guards to wait until morning at York's home until morning before beginning the trip Thus the three men had settled in for the historic night of February 28, 1884; Steele taking the first watch and guarding the handcuffed brave with a rifle, York retiring upstairs.

Late that night, a heavy knock on the door brought an unsuspecting Steele to his feet and, without thinking, he drew back the bolt. Suddenly, the door was thrown open, almost knockin him off he feet as ten men "faces blackened and red stripes painted around their eyes" forced their way into the room and disarmed him.

Upon hearing the commotion, York charged downstairs - when one of the grotesque invaders placed a cocked pistol to his head and rasped: "If you or your friend try to stop us, you'll get hurt."

Then, without further discussion, as the helpless constables stood meekly, one of the vigilantes knotted a rope around Louis Sam's wrist and jerked him to the door, where an estimated mob of 60 waited impatiently. Seconds later - after considerately promising to return the handcuffs - they were gone, helpless Sam striding to his fate without so much as a word or backward glance at York and Steele, who watched in anguish as the vigilantes disappeared in the night.

The mob was no sooner out of sight than they hurried to inform Mr. Campbell, who instantly galloped in pursuit with a posse of two Indians.

"About 168 or 169 paces taken from the boundary line," reported Cambell, "on this side of the line, I saw ... Louie Sam suspended by a rope from a tree. He was dead and cold. I got the two Indians to hold the body up and cut the rope and took it from around his neck ..."

It was the report of his recovery of Sam's body from the branch of a cedar tree on the Canadian side of the boundary that caused tempers to flare throughout British Columbia, the **Colonist's** editorial expressing the sentiments of many when it raged: "There is nothing brave, nothing

27

glorious and nothing just in the act of this band of lawless men. It was a cowardly and unwarranted deed . . . there is, there can be, no excuse for these - marauders to invade British soil and take the life of a man against whom at the worst only circumstantial evidence existed. They have not even the plea that British law miscarries like that of their own country. . .

"No matter in what light this foul murder is viewed, it should be regarded with the horror born of the knowledge that it was a lawless act committed under the cloak of meting out justice. It was not justice -- nothing can ever make it so -- and the hands of the lynchers are stained with blood; the possibility of the guilt of their victim serving nothing to wash away the stain. The murder of Mr. Bell was committed four miles this side of the border (sic) and the lynchers were Americans. For less than the deed they have done, serious international complications have arisen. The active participants and all those who tacitly abetted the crime by their presence, are not only lawbreakers, but murderers. They should be regarded with horror, and their conduct should meet with the severe punishment it justly merits."

Even Prime Minister Sir John A. Macdonald, in far-off Ottawa, was moved to note the affair in a letter to Governor General Lord Lansdowne, stating that although he knew the incident would "be much regretted in Washington, we may as well make it a matter of much importance - more especially as we get a complaint from there if a Canadian Indian happens to appropriate a horse or cow across the Frontier." If Macdonald's concern was motivated by something less than sympathy for Louis Sam, it did at least add federal weight, assuring that Sam's slaying would reach the highest corridors of power in the capitals of both nations.

Meanwhile, back in British Columbia, the tempo was increasing, passions warming with each new development in the case, even a non-development such as the Coroner's verdict. Held at Matsqui under the direction of Coroner C.

Todd, the inquest ruled that (no suprise) Louis Sam "came to his death by hanging, at the hands of a party of men believed to be from the American side."

A touch of intrigue was added to the case in 1949 when a magazine article mentioned a "mysterious charactger running through the evidence of that fateful night . . ." Unfortunately, little is known of this 'mysterious character', a bearded phanthom who allegedly had appeared at the York house earlier that day, requesting a meal and a bed. As was the custom of the day, he had been graciously satisfied on both counts. It apparently was believed by some, in view of later events, that this man was a spy, planted in the house to help the vigilantes gain admittance. However, this is the only reference to him.

Whatever, Louis Sam was dead, murdered at the hands of American vigilantes who had violated all that British justice held dear by seizing him from the arms of authority and unceremoniously dispatching him from the limb of a convenient cedar tree - on the Canadian side of the international boundary to boot.

While other newspapers took up the battle cry, castigating the federal government for what appeared to be its laxity in pursuing the case, detectives went into action in Washington Territory in a desperate bid to stave off what had all the signs of impending disaster: for members of Sam's tribe had called a council of war!

As armed bands of Indians galloped towards the Sumas reserve, detectives learned that the mob had been formed of residents of Lynken, Hogg's Prairie and Nootsack. The agents had no trouble in identifying the ringleaders who seemed in fact to be quite proud of their deed - one old man boasting to one and all that it had been his sons who led the mob that night.

On the Sumas reserve, the situation was fast approaching the crisis stage, the **Colonist** grimly warning: "They feel, as every right-minded white person must feel, than an outrage upon the laws, and through them the people,

This is the prospering British Columbia countryside just north of the Washington border, where, almost a century ago, the American vigilantes lynched poor Louis Sam.

has been committed. Their blood is up, and a revengeful blood it is when aroused and they are determined to effect a retaliation as fearful as the wrong that has been inflicted. Revenge, whatever purists may say to the contrary, is sweet to all; but to none more so than the Indian with whom it forms a part of his religion.''

Perhaps the factor which most incensed the Indians was that white man's justice had been impressed upon all Indians time and again, swiftly and severely. Now they demanded that the law prove itself - instantly. When finally the war council met, it came to a terrifying decision: to cross the border and hang the first white man they met in reprisal!

When word of this latest, chilling development swept the Northwest, Canadian and American authorities met in emergency sessions to discuss the worsening situation. Overnight, the tragedy had assumed horrendous proportions.

Ironically, for all of the two governments' concern and meetings, it remained for one dedicated civil servant to save the day. His name was Patrick McTiernan, 61 year olf Indian Agent who was responsible for the vast, rugged region south of and between Yale and Bute Inlet on the coast. Singlehandedly, he answered the greatest challenge of his career.

Demanding to meet with the assembled chiefs, as thousands of armed warriors continued to pour onto the reserve from every direction, McTiernan argued bravely that white man's justice would prevail. After hours of pleading and warning of the dire consequences, McTiernan and the chiefs reached a precarious agreement: they would wait just a little longer to see that his assurances were carried out. Then - if the American vigilantes still were not placed under arrest - they would storm the Washington border and a state of war would be in effect.

''Acts of violence, if allowed to pass unnoticed, but encourage their repitition,''another newspaper editorial warned the government, ''and the pressing need to suppress the vendetta that it seems is being inaugurated, is the

31

Pioneer Thomas Fraser York . . . as a young constable, he had faced a lunch mob . . .

first desideratum. How this will be done remains to be seen, but whatever action is taken, it is very certain, that to be effectual, promptness will have to be its chief characteristic.''

Incredible, - that's it. Overnight, the tempest abated, tempers cooled, the hanging of poor Louis Sam became a matter or record. The Sumas' threat of crossing the border en masse never came about, and sadly, the Washington murderers never faced a trial. The incident was simply closed.

Over a century later, we can but conjecture as to why the 'invasion' died so quickly - and why, in fact, it had arisen in the first place. One historian has given it as his belief that the lynching of Louis Sam had been the cuilmination of years of fear. Washington settlers, it seems, were forever apprehensive of attack by B.C. Indians and, to remove the threat once and for all, the more violent American element had approved a war of extermination on B.C. soil. According to this theory, Sam's hanging may have been a calculated attempt on the part of these whites to ignite a full-scale war which could only have ended with the decimation of the Sumas tribe and its allies.

Whatever the true cause, the incident died suddenly and irrevocably in anti-climax. It is ironic that, throughout the three weeks of international tension, the most important issue of all, that of Sam's guilt, seems to have been overlooked by all. Alas, even today, the mystery which sparked "one of the grossest outrages ever perpetrated in this province,"remains unsolved.

The evidence linking Sam with James Bell's murder is conflicting and circumstantial. According to one report, "the boots worn by the Indian, when captured, exactly correspond with the boot marks around Mr. Bell's house and that on him were found a knife and other articles which were recognized as having been in the store previous to the murder."

A second report states firmly that the only evidence against Sam had been the fact that he had "been seen on the road about a mile from Bell's farm and store."

Sam's tribesmen were vehement in their protests of his innocence, charging that the guilty man was an American telegraph linesman who had been seen galloping madly from the murder scene. More conclusive evidence, said the Sumas, had been found in the form of hoofprints surrounding the store, the linesman being "the only man who rode a shod horse in the vicinity." Indians and whites testified that, if nothing else, Bell had been unpopular with both races.

Ironically, the final scene of the tragic case of Louis Sam occurred years after when one-time special constable Thomas

33

Fraser York became customs and immigration officer at Huntingly, several miles from where he had faced the grotesquely painted lynch mob in 1884. While cleaning a lot for his new office, he uncovered a rusted gun barrel --none other than that which had belonged to Louis Sam. With the handcuffs Sam had worn to his death - which had been kept for 60 odd years by another pioneer family - Mrs. York turned the corroded barrel over to the Vancouver City Archives some 30 years ago.

And, on that incredible coincidence, the case of the lynching of Louis Sam was closed.

Remarkably, however, this is not the only instance in British Columbia history of vigilantes having taken justice into their hands. At least two other incidents have been recorded: the hanging of an old Indian by fiery American miners at Lytton in 1859 (his crime had been the theft of a loaf of bread), and the shotgun execution of 'One-Ear' Charley Brown, for the murder of a provincial constable some eight years later. This shooting actually occurred just across the international boundary when a posse had finally ambushed the rustler after a bitter manhunt.

THE FATAL FLIGHT
OF TRANS CANADA 810

By Frank W. Anderson

The terrible weekend that began on Saturday, December 8th, 1956, was one that would long be remembered acrosss western Canada in terms of pain, anguish and sorrow. It started with a gale force storm that swept over Vancouver Island, struck the mainland with devastating harshness and moved eastward over the mountains to assail the prairies. It ended with the mysterious disappearance of Trans Canada Flight 810 carrying 62 passengers and crew.

By four o'clock Sunday afternoon, however, the squall had passed and the skies over Vancouver's International Airport were clear and calm.

Captain Alan Jack Clarke, 35, was slated to take Trans Canada Flight 810 on its usual Sunday night run. A native of Montreal, he had joined the RCAF in 1940 and, after a brief posting with the force overseas, had been sent to Vancouver as an instructor on Liberty and Mitchell bombers. After the war, he had joined Trans Canada at Lethbridge, Alta.

Trans Canada Airlines had been established in April, 1937 and after two years of operation had begun passenger service across Canada on April 1, 1939. In later years, its name was changed to the now familiar Air Canada.

At Vancouver Airport, Captain Clarke was joined by his co-pilot, Terry Boon, and his stewardess, Dorothy Bjornsson, 24, who was filling in at the last moment for a sick comrade.

Flight 810 was a popular run for businessmen flying east for important Monday morning meetings, and many

The North Star, workhorse of the fleet

of the passengers who boarded that evening were salesmen and executives. Some were destined for cities as far east as Montreal. Many were returning home after seeing the first East-West Shrine football game played the day before at Empire Stadium.

A passenger with an unusual story was young, 18 year old Yuen Wan Woon. His family had previously made their ways from the interior of Red China to the freedom of Canada, leaving him trapped. By paying a substantial amount to underground agents, his father had arranged to have Yuen smuggled out of Communist China to Hong Kong where arrangements were made to fly him to Canada. Now, he was on the last leg of his adventure.

As in every major disaster, there were those w o Fate designated as 'lucky' and others as 'unlucky'. The case of the two McKays was a dramatic illustration. Larry McKay, of Winnipeg, had been to the coast on business and, hoping for a cancellation, had gone to the airport and obtained a stand-by ticket. Fortune seemed to be with him and at th last moment he was given permission to board the North Star. However, he had been seated only a few moments when Stewardess Bjornsson approached him ..... there had been a mistake ..... a mix-up in names .....the seat was reserved for another Mr. McKay. Larry left.

The second McKay was James McKay, of Calgary, who had planned to return home on the previous day but who had delayed his plans and booked to return home on the Sunday night flight. As his namesake departed, James McKay strapped himself into his seat, unaware that his destiny was soon to be fulfilled.

Flight 810 was over an hour behind schedule when it finally lifted off the runway of Vancouver's International airport and began to climb to its scheduled altitude of 19,000 feet. Its flight path would take it up the lower Fraser Valley to Hope and thence over the Selkirk and Rocky Mountain Ranges to Calgary.

On the way to Hope, Captain Clarke had a brief conversation with Captain Jack Wright, who was piloting a

Super Constellation into Vancouver from Toronto. Captain Wright reported that he had run into icing conditions and a 90 mile an hour wind over the Hope area and suggested that Clarke climb to 19,000 feet. Clarke responded that he was planning on that ceiling. The time was then 6:20 pm.

At 6:52, Captain Clarke reported to the Air Traffic Control in Vancouver that he had reached 19,000 feet and was levelling. A few minutes later, he was on the radio again, announcing that he was encountering severe turbulence at that altitude. He requested permission to climb to 21,000 feet and his request was granted immediately.

His plans to reach this altitude, however, never materialized. At that moment, a red warning light flashed on the instrument panel in front of him, indicating that there was either a fire or a 'hot spot' in Engine No. 2, the inner motor on the left wing of the four-motored craft. He cut the engine and feathered the prop to reduce wind resistance.

Though the North Star could navigate adequately on only three engines, Captain Clarke had two alternatives open in the event of further difficulty. He could continue on towards Calgary, relying on emergency airstrips at either Pentiction or Kimberley, or he could turn back and use the Abbotsford field in the event that he could not reach Vancouver.

At 6:57, he radioed: "We have just lost No. 2 engine. Holding 19,000. Endeavouring to maintain 19,000. We would like clearance immediately to get down if we can. We are losing altitude quite fast here."

Air Traffic Control then cleared him to descend to 14,000 feet. Here the first of several confusing radio transmissions took place, some of which were never satisfactorily explained.

"Is that for the Cultus Lake beam?" asked Clarke.

It was a strange question.

There were four main radio beams in the Vancouver and Cascade Mountain area. Green One, from Vancouver, extended east through Maple Ridge to Hope. Here it met the Princeton beam. About midway between Hope and Princeton, a third beam came up from Bellingham, Wash., and intersected with the Princeton beam. The fourth beam,

38

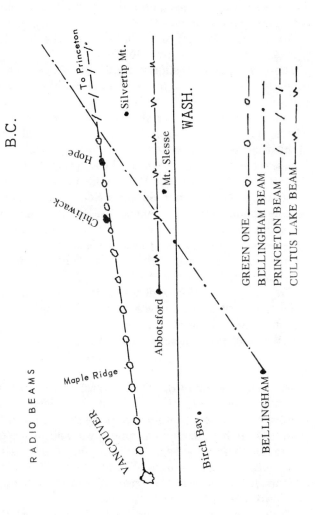

RADIO BEAMS

B.C.

WASH.

GREEN ONE ———o——o———
BELLINGHAM BEAM ——·——·——·——
PRINCETON BEAM ——/——/——/——
CULTUS LAKE BEAM ——ᴎ——ᴎ——

emanating from Abbotsford, extended eastward (almost paralleling Green One) and crossed the Bellingham signal at a spot almost due south of Chilliwack. This was the Cultus Lake beam and was almost 20 miles south of where Air Traffic Control assumed the North Star was battling the gale-force winds and sleet.

Air Traffic Control told him that it was for the Green One signal from Vancouver to Hope.

There was a radio silence until, at 7:01, Captain Clarke reported that he had passed Hope and was headed for Princeton. He noted that there was some evidence of ice forming on the wings and fuselage. He was cruising somewhere between 14,000 and 19,000 feet, well above the highest peaks in the region.

A few more minutes of struggling against the turbulence, the 90 mile an hour headwind, the increasing danger of icing and the loss of one engine evidently convinced Clarke that he should return to Vancouver. Before reaching Princeton, he put the North Star into a long, gradual turn and headed back. At 7:10 he made his last radio transmission to Air Traffic Control: "By Hope at 7:10, request descent to 10,000 feet."

The reply from Air Traffic Control was: "Roger. Clear radio range, cross Vancouver at 8,000 feet or above."

But , there was something radically wrong!. The North Star was not returning along Green One to Vancouver. It had veered away and was flying south west along the Bellingham beam.

The radar station at Birch Bay, Wash., familiarly known to pilots as Household Control, had the North Star on its scopes. "When the trouble report came in on Sunday night (that Clarke had lost an engine), we had the North Star on radar as it flew east. We tracked it from Hope to a point eight miles south of Princeton. Then it turned and headed back west. We tracked it as far as the vicinity of Silvertip Mountain. Then we lost it."

Though there were two radio systems aboard the North Star, repeated attempts by Air Traffic Control to contact the craft failed. Likewise, radio stations on the ground could not make any contact. In light of what was to follow, officials began to wonder whether both radios had been knocked out of commission by the turbulence or whether the crew was so busy coping with an unexpected menace that they did not have the opportunity to use their equipment.

At 7:20, assuming that all was well, Air Taffic Control sent out further landing instructions. There was no response.

At approximately 7:20 - ten minutes later - two ground observers noted something startling .....

Corporal Melford M. Henwood, 4th Field Squadron, stationed in the military barracks at Chilliwack, was in his car about five miles from town when his attention was drawn by a brilliant flash of light. "It was a million different colors," he told RCMP officers later. "It was about l0,000 feet uip up."

Henwood jumped from his car and watched. "Then the light disintegrated and began to fall. There were three red lights on it. Everything seemed to tumble down the sky."

The slower moving sound waves finally reached his ears and he heard the report of a tremendous explosion. As close as he could calculate, the light had landed in the vicinity of Mount Slesse, near the American border.

The time was approximately 7:30 on the evening of Sunday, December 9, 1956.

A few miles away, ham radio operator Gene Voight, who was hunting at Ryder Lake, also saw a mushrooming flash of pink and orange light in the mountain skies. It appeared to be about 20 miles away. He promptly drove a stake into the snow and took a compass reading. It was 110 degrees ESE from his position, somewhere in the vicinity of Silvertip Mountain. He also fixed the time at approximately 7:30.

It had been estimated by Air Traffic Control at Vancouver that the North Star would arrive over the airstrip at 7:28, but when that time passed and the craft was still not in sight, ATC notified the RCAF Search and Rescue squad at Sea Island base and asked them to "Stand by."

The continued radio silence from the airplane was disturbing.

The Search and Rescue Squad, under the command of Squadron Leader George Sheahan, contacted all radar stations in the district and in this way learned that Birch Bay had earlier tracked the missing North Star to the vicinity of Mt. Silvertip, 18 miles south-east of Hope. It was thus discovered that Captain Clarke was not on the assumed course along Green One.

The North Star had carried 1,760 gallons of fuel at takeoff and it was estimated that only about 300 gallons would have been consumed to this point. If Clarke had had to jettison his reserve fuel to maintain altitude, he would still carry enough to stay aloft until about 11 o'clock. With the reserve intact, he could extend that deadline until one o'clock.

At 8;35, with neither sight nor signal of the craft, Air Traffic Control advised Search and Rescue that Flight 810 was considered overdue. It asked for an air search in the hope that if the ship was still aloft, it could be guided into Vancouver by the search planes.

Two CF-100 fighter jets began to make a sweep of the path between Vancouver and Hope, but after several fruitless passes had to report that they had seen nothing in the air or on the ground.

By ten o'clock that evening, TCA officials began notifying the families of Captain Clarke, First Officer Boon and Stewardess Bjornsson that the North Star was overdue and the worst was feared. This news, however, was not released to the outside world or the relatives of the 59 passengers.

Over the next hour, more planes took to the air, widening the search area, "but in the darkness, there wasn't much we could see." The eleven o'clock deadline passed. There was only a glimmer of hope left ...

At 11:15, the airline officially announced that Flight 810 was overdue. The dire news was picked up by radio stations and thousands of people across Western Canada kept their radios on late into the night, picking up what scanty bits of information became available.

42

The search and rescue operation was closely linked with the RCMP detachments in the lower Fraser Valley and as early as 9:00 these had been alerted and the officers had begun to patrol the highways and side roads in search of information. In this way it was learned that several people had seen a flash of light or heard a tremendous explosion from the general direction of Silvertip Mountain. All seemed to place the time at around 7:30.

When dawn broke on Monday morning, 17 aircraft took to the skies in an urgent search for the missing craft. All knew that they had to locate the downed machine as quickly as possible for the sake of survivors - the North Star carried very little emergency equipment. They were disappointed, however, for scarcely had they taken off than the cloud level over the mountains descended as low as 3,000 feet and the air became exceedingly turbulent.

Since the reports of the two men who had seen an explosion near Mt. Slesse had not yet been received, the aircraft concentrated their efforts on trying to get close to Silvertip and other peaks in the vicinity. Unable to fly above the 3,000 foot level, their search was extremely unsatisfactory and no clues were found.

By mid-afternoon, with more reports coming in, the search broadened to include the Mt. Slesse area, but the low hanging clouds persisted. Search and Rescue were confident that if they could get only two hours of clear visibility, they could spot the wreckage.

Tuesday brought even more depressing news. Snow had begun to fall over the southern Cascade Mountains! While teams of experienced mountain climbers stood by with two nurses and two doctors, the pilots could only wait, hoping for a break in the weather.

It was about this time that Trans Canada authorities received disturbing news from Hong Kong. Mrs. Kwan Song, the wife of one of the passengers, informed police that her husband had been carrying nearly $80,000 in a money belt around his waist. After consultation with the RCMP, it was decided to keep this information secret lest the news lure ill-equipped and inexperienced mountain climbers into the area in quest of the missing fortune.

Wednesday, December 12, brought even more foul weather. All search planes were grounded.

Persistent reports reached headquarters that wreckage had been sighted on Sumas Mountain just outside of Chilliwack. An airial search had failed to locate the reported find. However, on Wednesday afternoon, two experienced climbers, accompanied by two reporters and Campbell Munro, brother of one of the ill-fated passengers, made their way up the 3,000 feet of exceedingly treacherous mountain side, only to find that the 'wreckage' was a group of rocks whose wet sides reflected the light.

That evening, when the weatherman forecast that there was no hope of a break in the weather, Search Leader George Sheahan decided to organize a ground search. On Thursday, he drove to Hope to put the plan into operation.

The ground arm of Search and Rescue was not very highly organized in 1956. It relied almost entirely on volunteers and borrowed equipment. Volunteers used their own transportation to get to base camps and supplied their own climbing equipment. RCMP and military personnel formed the backbone of such parties.

Food was donated by the merchants of Hope and a camp was set up at the junction of the Silver and Skagit Rivers. At dawn, Friday, Sergeant Tom Ferguson, RCMP, led a group of 32 men onto the lower slopes of Mt. Silvertip. Their job was to search as high as the tree line. If the weather cleared, members of the Alpine Club would be flown in to scour the upper reaches.

A second group, based at Vedder Crossing, undertook to search along the Chilliwack River in the direction of Chilliwack Lake. Like the first group, they carried provisions for two days and planned to scour as high as the treeline.

44

Late Friday evening, 14 members of the Alpine Club reached the Silvertip base camp to prepare for an assault on the upper reaches. Since the last radar contact had been in this vicinity, it was felt that the craft would be found there. There was no longer any hope that there would be survivors. Two feet of snow had already fallen in the area. Among these mountain climbers were four who were to figure prominently in the lang-drawn search. These were Fips Broda, Paddy Sherman, Elfrida Pigou and John Durda.

Saturday saw no progress. Fog, snow and rising winds made searching foolhardy.

On Sunday, with weather clearing somewhat, the mountain climbers attacked Mount Silvertip in earnest, probing into its uppermost reaches. Though they spent two days climbing, they located no trace of the vanished passenger plane. They were forced to conclude that it had not come down on that peak.

There were many false leads. An oil slick on Lake Chilliwack was explored; a landslide on another mountain was targetted - without luck. One appeared promising. Ralph Johnson, of Hope, reported hearing what seemed to be a human voice on a peak south of Silvertip. He and his party had not been able to reach the spot. The following day, a team of Alpine Club members investigated the report of the "voice on the mountain", but were forced to conclude that whatever Mr. Johnson and his friends had heard, it was not human.

With Silvertip eliminated, attention switched to the vicinity of Mt. Slesse and neighboring Mt. Rexford. By Monday night, two rescue teams had established base camps high up on both mountains.

That evening, a message was issued by Queen Elizabeth: "I have heard with deep concern of the tragic loss of the Canadian airliner in the Rocky Mountains. Please convey my sincere sympathy to all the relatives of those who have lost their lives."

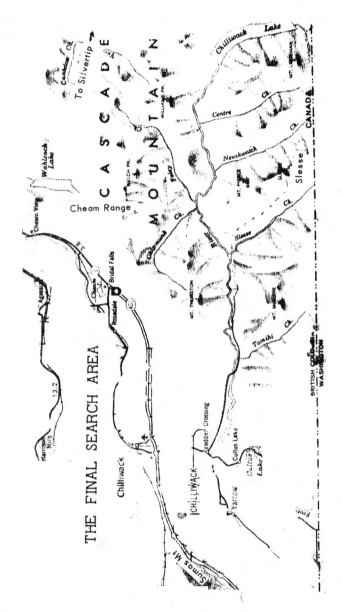

THE FINAL SEARCH AREA

By Wednesday evening, December 19, with continued bad weather hampering both land and air searches, the concerted effort was abandonned. Beyond the infrequent plane venturing over in ideal weather, it was felt that nothing could be done until the snows melted in the spring.

Just such a flight took place on the afternoon of December 24 when W.A. (Butch) Merrick took off from Abbotsford with Paul Martin as his observer. They flew east as far as Lake Chilliwack and then circled back. As they neared the east face of Mt. Slesse: "We saw it glittering in the sun. There was the shape of a fuselage and part of a propeller."

Both men saw it clearly. Merrick made a second pass at the crest of the mountain. "I got to within 50 yards of the peak and ledge," said Merrick. "I could see the shell hanging from a cable. Glittering pierces of fuselage There was absolutely no doubt in my mind about it."

In response to his call, a Search and Rescue plane took off from Vancouver and rendezvoused with him over the target. However, despite the fact that he led the search plane over the spot, observers aboard the craft, armed with binoculars, could see nothing. Later in the day, another private craft scouted the crest of Mt. Slesse but could only see what they took to be a tangle of trees - this despite the fact that the spot was at least 1500 feet above the treeline.!

While Merrick and Martin were certain that they had found the missing North Star, officialdom was not. The search was called off two days later.

As it eventually came about, the discovery of the wreckage came about by accident rather than planning.

On Saturday, May 11, 1957, five months after the North Star disappeared, Elfrida Pigou, Geoff Walker and David Cathcart left Vancouver to climb Mt. Slesse. Miss Pigou, who had been among the Alpine Club searchers in December, had climbed Slesse the previous year. They made camp in a deserted cabin at the 1,900 foot mark that night, preparatory for a Sunday climb.   47

48 *The tell-tale piece of wreckage that led to the discovery of*
Trans Canada Flight 810

Slesse was a rugged, 8,200 foot peak about two miles north of the American border. It had first been climbed in 1928, but it was not a popular peak and since then only some eight or nine parties had made the ascent. On February 20, 1955, Fips Broda and John Durda had made the first winter climb.

They moved out about 6 am on Sunday morning and began to climb the west slope. Their objective was an area known as the Circus, a notch between a large and smaller peak at the top. Cathcart, not feeling well, decided to stop before reaching the Circus, and the others went on alone. They met fog a little higher up and this slowed their progress.

"We had been climbing for six hours," Walker said later, "and we were just below two pinnacles of rock when I found a piece of paper lying in the snow." On examination, it proved to be a Trans Canada map of approaches to the airport at Sydney, N.S.!

Though hampered by fog and momentarily lost, they decided to push towards the Circus and regain their bearings. At the 7,300 foot mark, Elfrida found the first significant piece of evidence, a twisted piece of metal bearing a serial number. It was about three feet long. They were certain then that they had found the resting place of the North Star. It was 1:15.

With mixed emotions of elation and sadness, they searched around the Circus area and came upon more bits - a pressure fitting; some more twisted metal; then some pieces of cloth and upholstery. Unknown to them, the main wreckage was hidden by fog behind the south peak, only a few yards to the right and below them.

"We decided to pack down the largest piece," said Elfrida, "which was about three feet long. It was a bit awkward and sharp and jagged. It had numbers on it so they could make positive identification."

They did not reach their base camp until about eight o'clock in the evening and they paused there to have something to eat before starting the five mile hike to their car. Arriving back in Vancouver after two, they decided to wait until morning before notifying the authorities.

The first to be notified was Paddy Sherman, of **The Province** newspaper, an Alpine Club colleague of Pigou and one who had spent many hours searching for the North Star. He took the jagged fragment of metal to Vancouver Airport where, within minutes, it was identified as part of the underside of a wing of the missing plane.

The general public first learned of the discovery when an extra edition of **The Province** hit the streets at noon.

During the winter, there had been unconfirmed reports of Kwan Song and his missing $80,000, and fearing that the announced discovery of the North Star might spur amateurs into trying to scale treacherous Mt. Slesse, George Sheahan of Search and Rescue alerted the RCMP and roadblocks were immediately set up, blocking the road to Slesse.

The problem facing Search and Rescue now was the feasibility of retrieving the bodies from the mountain top and an examination of the pattern of the wreckage in search of clues that might explain the mid-air explosion and crash. There was no longer any need for extreme haste.

A scan of the crash site from a helicopter showed that the North Star had crashed on the east face of the south peak of Mt. Slesse. It appeared to have come almost straight down, rather than running into the side of the slope. Since there was no place that a helicopter could land, the closest approach would have to be to land men on a ledge farther down on the less difficult west side, from where they could climb to the crash site.

In view of the scanty information that could be derived from this report, Coroner Glen McDonald, of Vancouver, announced that he would be satisfied if only one body could be retrieved. A presumption of the deaths of the remaining 61 persons could then be made from that fact. Since his office had collected the dental charts of nearly all the passengers and crew, it was hoped that the identification process would be simplified.

An engine perched precariously on the steep slope

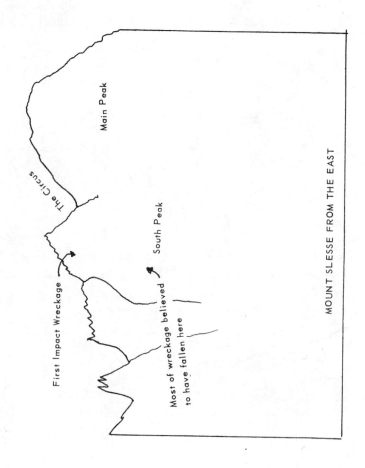

The Circus

First Impact Wreckage

Main Peak

South Peak

Most of wreckage believed
to have fallen here

MOUNT SLESSE FROM THE EAST

52

Later in the day, with mist shrouding the mountain, a base camp was set up at the junction of the Slesse and Chilliwack Rivers and members of the Alpine Club were flown there to wait for clearer weather. Among them were Elfrida Pigou, Fips Broda, John Durda and Paddy Sherman.

Tuesday, May 14, dawned clear and calm. It was an ideal day for climbing, but a grim day for exploration. An airial survey had shown that the main body of wreck age lay some 100 feet below the crest of the south peak. It was assumed that the main portion had slithered down the east face for some 2,000 feet or so and was probably in a heavily snowed-in section. Consequently, the climbers were divided into two groups.

One party, consisting of Fips Broda, Elfrida Pigou, John Durda and Paddy Sherman were airlifted by an RCAF Piasecki helicopter to the 5,700 foot level. While the craft balanced with the tips of its runners on a narrow ledge, the four made their way to the rock surface. Their instructions from George Sheahan were to try to locate any bodies for identification and, secondly, to ascertain the best route by which to bring in a party of engineers and technicians from Trans Canada and the Department of Transport who could try to piece together the cause of the disaster. In order to assist this process, the team was asked to return any pieces of metal they moved in their search for bodies to the exact position in which they found them.

The second set of climbers, including Jack Russel, Ian Kay, Roy Mason, Joe Hutton and Russell Yard, was to work its way along the east face of Slesse some 2,000 feet below the point of impact and try to locate bodies or more pieces of the wreckage.

Working their way up the 40 degree slope with picks and ropes, the four Alpinists attained the Circus, or saddle, from where they could obtain a clear view of the disaster. There was a large black mark where the plane had impacted and the force of the crash had loosened rocks for some distance around. Oil from the four engines had left slippery patches that were treacherous underfoot. Some of the wreck-

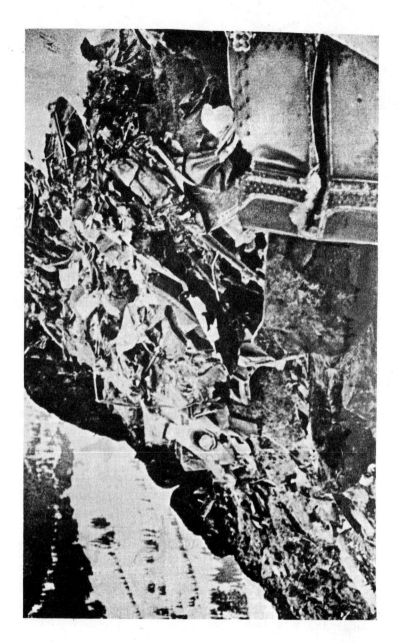

age, such as the pieces found by Pigou and Walker, had been flung forward onto the surface of the Circus.

Below the impact point was part of the fuselage. Steel cables leading from it to the wing had snagged on some rocks and prevented it from slithering down the east face.

Fips Broda told me later: "One only has to see the wreck to know that no one could have lived even a fraction of a second after the crash."

Working their way down across the slope, they became conscious of the sweet smell of decaying flesh. Elfrida Pigou had to turn back. The other three made their way cautiously over the slippery rocks, passing under the fuselage until they could reach a relatively secure area above it. As they went under the cabin, they could see the half-body of a man in a TCA uniform suspended inside.

The three men were working on an exceedingly steep and uncertain slope and several times, as helicopters hovered nearby, they had to desperately wave them back, afraid that the vibrations of the rotors would loosen the shattered rock face and send them hurtling 2,000 feet straight down.

Unable to get to the suspended cabin of the plane, they had to make a decision. There was a portion of an engine with a bent propeller on it perched on an out-cropping and Fips Broda volunteered to try to cross the rock face and reach it. "I wanted to look at the serial number," Mr. Broda told the author in a 1979 interview in Vancouver, "to make sure, because we were asked down below to make sure that we brought some fact back."

With Sherman belaying him, Broda worked his way carefully across the open space to the engine, "I have seen during the war some pretty gruesome scenes, but I've never seen a mangled mass like that," he continued. "Especially when it's decomposed for about five or six months. At the front during the war, you see dead bodies - you see them sometimes mangled too - maybe more than just one in a heap - but there were the remnants of some 62 people which was different and I had to walk over that - partly covered by snow but partially open

Waldemar 'Fips' Broda Today

First Impact Wreckage

The Circus

South Peak

Main Peak

Most of wreckage believed
to have fallen here

Nesakwatch River Valley

MOUNT SLESSE FROM THE EAST

already due to the heat of the sun burning down. That alone is something you feel quite unhappy about. It is not a nice experience at all.''

In places, Fips Broda found that small pieces of wreckage were lightly embedded in the rock and could be dislodged by a flick of the finger - further confirmation that the North Star had fallen onto the mountain, rather than smashing into it at full speed.

When he reached the engine perched on the knoll, he touched it for support, but it immediately slid about eight inches down the slope. He gave up the attempt and worked his way back across the uncertain rock surface to his companions.

In a final attempt to obtain positive identification, Paddy Sherman and John Durda lowered Broda on a rope until he was able to reach into the shattered cabin and remove the wallet from the pocket of the half-man suspended inside. This, together with some pieces of mail that were surprisingly clean and intact, formed the sum of their efforts. They then made their ways back down the mountain to rendezvous with the helicopter that took them to base camp.

While they were engaged in their extremely perilous task, others - less experienced and less well-equipped - were trying to fight their way through the deep snows of the mountainside. Two were taken off by helicopter. An RCMP officer was quoted: ''They must have been nuts.''

News of the $80,000 money belt had spread quickly and over the next few days the police searched every car at the barricade. Some carried climbing equipment!

An inquest opened that night in the city police courtroom in Chilliwack and both parties made their reports. The second group of climbers related that while they had found numerous pieces of wreckage, they had not located any bodies. Their search had been hampered by snow which in some places was still ten to fifteen feet deep. The first group, after telling of their difficulties at the crash site, suggested that it would be impossible to bring out even part of a body for identification. Coroner McDonald made no friends when he wondered if experienced Alpine climbers from Switzerland or Austria should not be brought in to accomplish this seemingly simple task!

The inquest concluded the following day with the understanding that, until the snows had been melted, no more attempts would be made to reach the mountain top. The RCMP would continue its surveillance around the base of Mt. Slesse to ensure that foolhardy climbers would not go searching for the reputed money belt, and a public warning was issued that tampering with the site could bring a fine of $5,000 and/or a year in jail.

Several commissions had been set up to inquire into the cause of the terrible disaster and one of these was headed by Desmond Murphy, 56 year old superintendent of air operations for the Department of Transport. Determined to reach the site of the disaster, but being unable to climb, he approached Fips Broda and asked for a crash course in climbing. Impressed with his dedication, Broda agreed and enlisted the assistance of his friend, Paddy Sherman. Over the next few weeks, with Sherman doing most of the instructing, Desmond Murphy haunted the slopes of Grouse Mountain. Occasionally Fips Broda would join them and the three would practice rope climbing.

In preparation for a public inquiry that was to open in July, Desmond, Broda and Sherman were flown to Mt. Slesse by RCAF Piasecki helicopter and set down on the precarious ledge at the 5,700 foot level.

Roped between the two experienced man, Murphy bravely and skillfully made the climb. It was a dangerous ascent, for rock broke off in their hands as they sought to find and maintain holds, but when they reached the Circus and crossed over to the wreck, a sweet odor still lingered in the air.

There was little fresh evidence. The shattered fuselage, about 15 feet remaining, hung from its cables and the fragments of engines and propellers still clung to precarious perches on the almost sheer slope. They did find two bundles of letters and two wallets - one belonging to Brigadier H.W. Wright and the other to Miss Jean Grant. There was no trace of Kwan Song and the missing money belt.

After spending some time photographing the scene so that graphic evidence could be included with his report to the Department of Transport in Ottawa, Desmond Murphy indicated that he had accomplished all he could and the three men made their way back down to the 5,700 foot ledge where the helicopter eased in to pluck them off.

When the public inquiry opened in the second week of July, a minimum of evidence was introduced. Desmond Murphy testified, citing from the log reports of Air Traffic Control. The meagre story that emerged was that the North Star had lost an engine and was returning to Vancouver when the disaster took place. Why Captain Clarke did not, or could not, maintain radio contact with his home base remained an enigma. From other testimony, it seemed evident that an explosion of some sort had taken place in mid-air, but there were no clues as to the origin of the blast. Gasoline? A bomb? No one would ever know. The pattern of wreckage on the east face of Mount Slesse's south peak indicated only that the North Star had fluttered down to earth.

Said lawyer Ian A. Snow, one of the ten attorneys to appear on behalf of suits filed by relatives of the passengers: "The authorities showed the greatest reluctance to introduce material." The truth of the matter was that there was little evidence to put in. The last radio contact with Capt. Clarke had been at 7:10. The flash of the explosion had been reported by Corporal Henwood and Jean Voight as taking place at approximately 7:30. There was nothing that even hinted at what might have transpired aboard Flight 810 during those crucial 20 minutes. Those moments were locked in the now-dead memories of the 62 passengers and crew.

As the first anniversary of the air disaster approached, Trans Canada Airlines erected a beautiful, eight foot granite monument near the south bank of the Chilliwack River, some 20 miles from Mount Slesse. Inscribed on the bronze plaque were the names of the 62 victims. At an estimated cost of $30,000, it flew in relatives from as far away as Florida, New York and Montreal.

On Monday, December 9, 1957, with brilliant sunlight casting dark shadows across the scene, some 350 spectators gathered to participate in the memorial service. Today, one can still drive to the monument and stand in reverence amid the trees and mountains.

Of those who participated in the search and eventual discovery of the North Star, many are no longer alive. Desmond Murphy, the inspector of the Department of Transport, collapsed at his desk a year later and died of a heart attack. Miss Elfrida Pigou, together with three companions, lost her life in an avalance on Tiedemann Glacier, Mount Waddington, on July 30 or 31, 1960.

John Durda, one of the four who first reached the ill-fated passenger plane, was killed in the mid 1960s when his light aircraft crashed in the Fraser River mud flats. W.T. (Butch) Merrick, who first sighted the wreckage on Mount Slesse, died at Abbotsford on January 2, 1979.

Others, such as Fips Broda, Hal Fryer and Dave Archer - who helped greatly in the gathering of information and the unravelling of technicalities in this story - still retain vivid memories of their roles in the fatal flight of 810.

My thanks are due to Lyle and May Howarth, Coquitlam, B.C.; Harold Fryer, Salt Spring Island; and Dave and Norma Archer, of Enderby, B.C., for their technical assistance and first hand knowledge of the communications problems of Flight 810. A separate mention is worthy of the help rendered by Waldemar Fips Broad, Vancouver, whose narrative of the search for evidence at the crash site was of the utmost importance in understanding that section of events.

Photographs of the crash were kindly made available through Paddy Sherman, publisher of **The Province.**

Who Killed Dick Vadnais?

The following cryptic paragraph appeared in the Annual Report of Commissioner Aylesworth Bowen Perry of the Royal North West Mounted Police for the year 1909:

"Nolle Prosequi. The accused Eloise Vadnais, wife of Richard Vadnais, stood here jointly charged with one Theodule Bissette, for the attempted murder of her husband. After the disposal of this case another attempt was made on the life of Richard Vadnais, resulting fatally."

The beautiful rolling foothills of Boundary Creek, N.W.T., tucked away in the remoteness of southwestern Alberta, attracted many types of settlers at the turn of the century. Some came, like those of the Mormon faith, seeking a new home and a refuge from persecution. Others, seeking after the elusive lost gold mine on Chief Mountain, built log cabins in the hills and went mysteriously about their secretive business. Stil more eyed the ground and dreamed of acres of flowing wheat. A few, like Richard Vadnais, thought in terms of ranching.

Better known as Dick Vadnais, the man from Quebec appeared on the old western scene around 1890 as a cowhand, cum whiskey trader, in Montana Territory. Joe Vadnais, a sharp-minded oldster of 81 years living at Cardston today, related that in 1902 he helped Dick drive his first herd into Canada from Montana to establish a ranch one mile north of Carway.

Dick was, in the opinion of Joe Vadnais, "one of the best damned ranchers to settle in this part of the country." He was also, in the mind of Staff Sergeant John S. Piper, RNWMP, a man who created many problems for himself for his fondness for liquor and his short-fused temper.

He married Eloise Bissette, a French Canadian girl with a temper to match his own and a gun-slinging ability

The Old Hendry Ranch at Boundary Creek

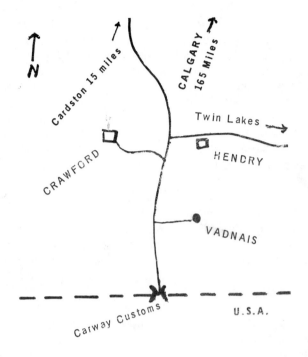

that was the envy of many a cowpoke. They had one child, a boy of shy demeanour and extremely sensitive temperament, and a daughter of religious inclination who entered a convent in Lethbridge at an early age.

The strange drama began on the night of August 24, 1908, when Richard Vadnais arrived home from Cardston with a stomach full of liquor and found his brother-in-law, Theodule Bissette in the ranch house. For some time there had been rough quarreling between Dick and his equally quick-tempered wife about the continued presence of her brother at the ranch, and upon seeing him there Vadnais became angry and tried to throw him out bodily.

According to testimony later related, Bissette drew a knife, whereupon Vadnais ran out of the house and picked up a piece of scantling to use as a club.

As he re-approached the house to enter the kitchen, he was met at the door by Bissette who levelled a .32 pocket revolver at him and pulled the trigger. The single bullet caught him in the chest and spun him.

Despite this wound, Vadnais - who stood six foot four and had the strength of an ox - ran to the corrals about 125 yards north of the house with the obvious intent of saddling a horse. However, seeing that Bissette and his wife Eloise (also armed) were close behind him, he changed his plan and continued to run north towards the ranch of a neighbor - Hendry.

It was a terrifying run of half a mile!

At one point the lumbering giant stumbled and crashed to the ground. This enabled Bissette and the woman to overtake him. Here a second shot was fired at him - the bullet glancing from his right wrist and plowing through the forearm. Vadnais struggled to his feet and continued his headlong flight.

Alerted by the sound of the second shot, Old Man Hendry and his two sons came out of their yard just in time to see Vadnais scramble over the barbed wire fence.

In mortal fear of his life, Dick seized Mr. Hendry and tried to hold him between himself and his assailants. Seeing that the murderous pair were not following up their attack, Hendry was able to escort Vadnais to a granary and make him comfortable on some robes. Not wishing to lose sight of their quarry, Bissette and Eloise followed them inside.

Mr. Henry, after dispatching one of his sons to a neighboring ranch - that of Vernon Shaw - stood guard in the granary.

Vernon Shaw rode to the Twin Lakes detachment to notify Corporal Miles of the RNWMP.

Miles, who was alone at the detachment, deputized Shaw and returned with him to the Hendry ranch.

On entering the granary, Corp. Miles found Dick Vadnais lying on the floor with Mrs. Vadnais standing guard over him with a .44 revolver in her hand. She greeted

Vernon Shaw

him with: "I want a doctor for this man. I shoot to protect myself."

Miles disarmed her and then searched Theo Bissette, who was standing nearby. From the man's pocket he extracted a .32 revolver. Each gun later proved to contain one discharged shell.

After placing the brother and sister under arrest for the attempted murder of Richard Vadnais, Corporal Miles arranged for transportation of the trio to Cardston, 15 miles north, where the wounded man was given over to the care of Dr. Stackpoole.

With that deceptively smooth swiftness of Canadian justice on the frontier, the preliminary hearing opened in Cardston on the afternoon of Saturday, August 29. The pros-

67

ecution was conducted by Corporal Miles, while the famous and controversial lawyer, Paddy Nolan, of Calgary, sat at the defense table.

Corporal Miles was the first to give evidence and he was followed on the stand by Dr. Stackpoole. The medical testimony was simple and in everyday English. One bullet had struck Vadnais in the right forearm and had passed through just above the wrist. The second, a .44, had struck the third rib on the left side and lodged in the muscles of the arm. Had it not been deflected from the rib, it would have been fatal.

The third witness on the stand was a French Canadian ranch hand from the Vadnais place who spoke no English. Inspector Thomas Sherlock Belcher, before whom the case was being conducted, adjourned the hearing while a search was made for an interpretor.

Finally, Miss Stewart, a local teacher, was prevailed to reluctantly act.

Through this witness, it was learned that the extent of the Vadnais' in-law problem was greater than had been appreciated. In addition to Theo Bissette and his family of seven, a sister of Mrs. Vadnais was also living in the large, two-storey farm house a mile north of the Customs at Carway.

Having been a witness to the first shot, he outlined the sequence of events as given here. He was replaced on the stand by Vadnais himself, who added little that was new. At the conclusion of the testimony, Inspector Belcher bound both the accused over for trial.

Theodule Bissette was taken to the main prison at Calgary, operated by the RNWMP, while his sister was released on a $2,000 bail put up by her erstwhile target! That evening, she returned to the ranch in company with her husband and her two children, Flossie and Willie.

With this sort of fraternization between victim and accused, it was a foregone conclusion that the case would fizzle out and all would be forgiven - if not forgotten. This proved true. The evidence given at the trial was so confused and vauge that the brother and sister were acquitted. There was one bri. ht event, however, Theodule Bissette and his family moved out, as did the sister-in-law, so that the Vadnais could at least try to work out their problems together.

The tempestuous nature of both Eloise Vadnais, who was short and plump, and her large, raw-mannered husband, did not make them sociable neighbors, despite the gatherings held frequently at the big house (which was the only two storey home at Boundary Creek.) Consequently, the pair had many acquaintances, but no close friends. Turmoil seemed a daily routine in their lives.

Richard Vadnais was suspected of being a whiskey runner, which made his farm a constant - though futile - target for raids by the police. In addition, he was constantly having branding problems with an American rancher who lived just across the line - Percy de Wolff.

Percy de Wolff - or as the police records say Percy DeWolfe - had been responsible for some hanky-panky with horse-stealing back in 1901. He and several Canadian accomplices had been responsible for stealing large numbers of Canadian animals and spiriting them across the border to the de Wolff Ranch, from whence they were sold to American farmers. With the help of a Canadian rancher - name witheld by the police, Supt. Richard Burton Deane had cracked the ring and was responsible for de Wolff collecting a ten year term in Deer Lodge Penitentiary. De Wolff got out early for good behaviour.

An interesting story about the quick-draw and shooting ability of de Wolff with a sixgun was told to the author by Freeman Cook of Boundary Creek. Challenged to take a shot at a sparrow some distance away, Percy drew and fired with one smooth motion and picked off the unsuspecting target.

This, then, was the man with whom Richard Vadnais was having some problems about mis-branding of stock.

However, when in the early morning hours of January 30, 1909, word was brought to the Mounted Police headquarters at Cardston that there had been another shooting at the Boundary Creek ranch, the first thought which crossed official minds was that the domestic quarrel had broken out anew.

Detective Sergeant John S. Piper was placed in charge of the investigation and he proceeded to the ranch. He found that one window of the kitchen had been shattered. The glass had been blown inward onto the floor. There were black marks on the window pane and later, upon analysis, these proved to be gun powder grains.

Dick Vadnais had been shot at the kitchen table, and by tracing the probable path of the two bullets which struck him, Piper unearthed a misshapen slug embedded in the kitchen wall. It was too distorted to determine either the make or calibre.

Outside the kitchen window, where the snow was trampled by the sniper's feet, he found a bullet casing from a rifle. The casing bore a U.S. Government stamp.

A thorough search of the house turned up only one weapon, a hunting rifle in a case. It had not been discharged for some time.

The shooting had taken place about eleven o'clock on Saturday evening. Two bullets, fired closely together, had struck Richard Vadnais in the lower portion of his face. The marksman had obviously been shooting to kill. Momentarily stunned, Vadnais had recovered his balance and ran out of the house. With incredible strength and stamina, he had gone first to the granary and taken down a heavy stock saddle. He then toted it to the corral, 125 yards away. Here he saddled a horse and rode to the ranch of a Mr. Crawford about a mile to the northwest.

From thence, he was driven by light democrat to the hospital at Cardston by Messrs. Crawford and Salt.

When Det. Sgt. Piper interviewed the wounded man in the Cardston Hospital he found that Dick Vadnais was unable to talk. When Piper asked if he knew who shot him, Vadnais pointed to his wife, who was present in the room. Piper automatically assumed that the gesture meant that she had fired the shots through the window.

When Eloise Vadnais left the hospital room later in the day, she was arrested for the attempted murder of her husband. She scoffed at the idea and refused to make a statement or to answer any questions. In the face of her silence, Piper could only have her transported to Calgary and lodged in the women's section of the Mounted Police prison.

On Monday, February 1, as Richard Vadnais's condition was deteriorating and the aggravation of his wounds seemed to affect his ability to think clearly, he was taken by train to the Galt Hospital in Lethbridge, accompanied by Dr. Stackpoole.

It appeared that Vadnais' rugged constitution was going to succumb to this second attempt on his life, and Inspector Harfield West decided to take drastic action. He had the Crown Prosecutor draw up a series of questions about the shooting which could be answered Yes or No by nodding or shaking the head.

The visit of Inspector West, who had known the big Frenchman officially and unofficially for nearly 18 years, was a strange encounter. West had been present in the room during the first brief interview at the Cardson Hospital and had seen Dick point to his wife in response to the question: "Who shot you?" He was, therefore, psychologically geared to hear evidence and details corroborating Mrs. Vadnais' guilt, rather than to hold an open inquiry. He knew, also, from reports of the doctors at the hospital that the 45 year old rancher sometimes suffered from spells of delerium brought on by a spreading infection from the two bullet wounds that had carried away his tongue and much of his mouth.

It was not, thus, until much later that the full significance of some of the imformation obtained from him was realized.

Unable to talk or write, Dick Vadnais outlined the events in the tragic story., He indicated that he, his wife and

71

son, Willie, were seated at the kitchen table, eating a late meal, when the shots were fired. He also drew his own stock brand, a Lazy Candlestick, on a piece of paper. Beside, it, he drew another brand, a Leaning Candlestick. He seemed quite agitated during this phase of the interview, but was unable to make his concerns clear to Inspector West.

The interview ended uncertainly, with each man taking away a different interpretation.

The condition of Dick Vadnais deteriorated steadily. There were periods of lucid thinking, but these became shorter and farther apart. More and more, both his thinking and behaviour became irrational. By February 19, it became obvious to both doctor and patient that the murderous bullets had done their deadly job. At his request, his wife was brought to see him.

With the police present, and using the strange sign language, Vadnais cleared his wife of any complicity. He died of his wounds at one o'clock on the morning of Saturday, February 20, 1909.

An inquest was inevitable, but now it was to be a hearing with a totally new focus. Rather than: ''Why did Eloise Vadnais kill her husband?'', the question now was: ''Who killed Dick Vadnais?''

The inquest was convened by Coroner Gould, of Pincher Creek, on the evening of Vadnais' death. A jury was assembled under foreman J.L. Manwaring, and after viewing the body adjourned to the next Wednesday.

Some interesting problems were presented as witnesses gave their evidence. Several witnesses said that Vadnais, when first asked if his wife had shot him, had nodded affirmatively. Against this was his death bed declaration exonerating her, plus the statement that she was at the kitchen table when the shots came from outside.

Vadnais had attempted, also, with some agitation to convey a message concerning the Lazy Candlestick and Leaning Candlestick stock brands. This aspect took on an added meaning when one of the ranch hands testified that Vadnais had been having some difficulty with an American rancher who ran the latter brand. Another police witness testified that several of the cattle on the Vadnais spread carried both brands! The unanswered question was: Who had added the extra brand, Vadnais or his American neighbor?

Detective Sergeant Piper brought out a salient piece of information which raised only one more question mark. Relating that the Vadnais' home stood on a small hill and that the ground around it was devoid of trees or cover, he gave as his opinion - since it had been a clear night with the moonlight reflected well from a cover of snow - that no person could have gotten away from the ranch house without being seen by Vadnais, his wife or son.

The star witness on the second day of the inquest was seven year old Willie Vadnais. By common agreement it was decided that he would be examined by the famed Paddy Nolan, who was representing the interests of Mrs. Vadnais.

Willie's testimony, given in response to a series of short-answer questions, was routine up to the point of the shooting. He indicated that he was sitting at the kitchen table, eating soup with his father and mother. Then -- and he clapped his hands sharply twice -- the shots came. He said his father and mother then ran outside.

The Crown's questions, while penetrating, were not distressing to the boy and did nothing to alter his story. In the end, he had merely corroborated the account given by his father.

Despite the stories of father and son, Detective Sergeant Piper still had his doubts. He was convinced that no one could have gotten away from the Vadnais house that evening without being seen, yet, Eloise Vadnais - according to the testimony of her son - had run outside immediately after the shots. Surely she would have seen such a person. The crucial question was why she now refused to make any statement at all. Was she protecting someone from love or fear, or was the simple truth that no such person existed

Patrick James Nolan (1864-1913) who watched over Eloise Vadnais' interests, was one of the most famous Canadian trial lawyers. Educated in Ireland, he was called to the bar of the North West Territories in 1889.

Det. Sgt. John Piper

and that Vadnais and the boy were sheltering her. Piper leaned to the latter view.

The inquest ended with the verdict, read by the foreman of the jury, Mr. Manwaring, that Richard Vadnais had come to his death "from a gun in the hands of some person or persons unknown."

Having come this far with the theory that Mrs. Vadnais had murdered her husband, it was difficult for the police to return and begin searching again in a new direction. Consequently all charges against the energetic little lady were withdrawn and she was freed to return to the ranch.

Today, the old two-storey Vadnais ranch house no longer overlooks the beautiful basin of treeless prairie nestled across the Canada-U.S. border. Mrs. Vadnais left it shortly after her release and returned to the United States. For some time after her departure, it was found impossible to rent or sell the property because of the unhealthy memories connected with it. When, eventually, it did find a purchaser, ill-luck still attended. A mysterious fire did serious damage to the outside of the house and a later fire destroyed it completely. Finally, the land was acquired by Eric Luther, who in turn sold the farm to its present owners, Mr. and Mrs. Royce Cook. Today, a modern highway built in the 1940s has supplanted the old trail that ran past the farm to Cardston.

It is said that Willie Vadnais returned to the old farm for a brief visit in the late 1920s and wandered around the old corrals and out-buildings, but Mrs. Vadnais never returned to the scene of the mysterious stragedy. Today, only Chief Mountain remains to look majestically down upon the basin - as he did that night so many years ago when *somebody murdered Dick Vadnais.*

The Sadness of The Willow Bunch Giant

The folklore of the world abounds in tales of mythical giants who roamed the planet at various times - most notable of whom was Goliath whose earliest reported height was six cubits and a span, or approximately 9 feet, six inches. Later data puts this at a mere 6 feet 10. There have been many others, some dating from the Middle Ages and others from remote regions of the world. All have one thing in common - their heights are usually exaggerated by 12 to 18 inches.

Medical science recognizes two types of giants; those who are "normal" and whose height is the result of heredity and environment; and the pathological giants whose height is the result of an over-active pituitary gland. The **Guinness Book of World Records** rates Angus MacAskill of Scotland as the tallest normal giant. Born in 1825, MacAskill imigrated to Nova Scotia and lived most of his life on Cape Breton Island. On his death in 1863, his height was recorded at 7 feet 9 inches.

There is ample medical evidence at present to award the title of tallest man to Robert Waldow, born at Alton, Illinois on February 22, 1918. On his death in 1940, he stood 8 feet and 11 inches and weighed 439 pounds. Second in line is John F. Carroll, of Buffalo, N.Y., whose recorded height was 8' 7-3/4''. Carroll died in 1969 at the age of 37. The third tallest man is listed at 8 feet 6 inches in stature. He was John William Rogan, of Gallatin, Tennessee, who died in 1905.

Strangely, Edouard Beaupre, of Willow Bunch, Saskatchewan, does not appear in the Guinness list of tallest men, though there is irrefutable evidence that he was the fourth tallest man on record. Edouard's verified height at death was 8 feet 3 inches. Instead, the **Guinness Book of**

Top Left - Mr. Lapointe; Lower Left - Louis Legare
Edouard Beaupre
Right - Gaspard Beaupre, father

On Wednesday, July 4, 1990, the ashes of Edouard Beaupre arrived in Willow Bunch after an absence of 92 years. For years his naked skeleton had lain on display at the University of Montreal. Following a relentless campaign for repatriation by Ovila Lesperance and Cecile Gibouleau, the University finally relinquished its dubious claim to the remains. After cremation, his ashes were interred in front of the Willow Bunch Museum beside a new statue of the celebrated giant. Over 100 relatives attended.

Records lists the fourt tallest man as Dan Keohler, of Denton, Montana, who died in 1973. His height is given as 8 feet 2 inches.

The saga of Edouard Beaupre, the Willow Bunch Giant, is a simple - but a sad one. His father, Gaspard Beaupre, was a Red River Metis who came west to the Wood Mountain area in the late 1870s and settled in the tiny community of West Willow Bunch in the North West Territories. Indians had long wintered along the Missouri Couteau, and with the coming of the white fur traders they had set up rendezvous points at Wood Mountain.

Among these fur traders was Louis Legare, who was later to gain fame as a police scout and as a confidant of the American Sioux Chief, Sitting Bull. He founded West Willow Bunch, sometimes called Fort Legare. Another Red River Metis, Trefle Bonneau, a rancher, presided over another miniature village called East Willow Bunch. Later, these two settlements merged into one and established a school and church. The country was composed of rolling hills covered with sage and short grass - ideal for cattle, horse thieves and nature lovers.

It was here that Gaspard Beaupre settled and here that he met and married Florestine Piche, a local Metisse girl. Both were devout Catholics and faithful attenders at the little church operated by Father St. Germain, O.M.I.

Writing in the Autumn issue of **Saskatchewan History** August Dahlman recounts a quaint story about Florestine Beaupre: "Legend says that before his birth his Indian (sic) mother was picking Saskatoons and wished always that she was tall enough to reach those better berries at the top of the tree." Whether this be true or not, her wish was to be fulfilled in a roundabout way with the birth of her first child, Joseph Edouard, on January 9, 1881.

There was nothing unusual about Edouard at birth. He weighed 9 pounds and was normal in every respect. His parents were also average, with Gaspard standing at 5 feet 8 inches and his wife, Florestine, measuring 5 feet 4.

79

Young Edouard grew normally until the age of three, though he was a very active boy with an inquisitive nature and a large appetite. Then, his pituitary gland began to act up and in response he began to grow at an alarming pace. By the time he was ready for school, he was as big as his teacher, and by the age of nine he stood six feet.

Unfortunately, almost as if his total vigor was going to sustain his abnormal growth, his being was suffering in other ways. The unexpected drain on his energy seemed to affect his ability to learn and his progress at school was slow. He missed a great deal of the classes, a process which in itself handicapped him. Also, as his height increased, he grew more and more different from his classmates and this distinction made attendance at school harder for him. It was no suprise, then, that he attended less frequently and that before long he dropped his studies.

Children of normal proportions have difficulty in their teen years coping with the sudden growth of that period and their attempts to adjust to their rapidly changing bodies results in awkwardness and seld-consciousness. With Edouard, this process was even more drastic since he changed so rapidly. He was constantly in a state of adjustment and never seemed to win the battle against his awkwardness. As Dr. Jean Maurice Blais later noted: "He demonstrated a dazed state of mind almost constantly." It must have been a terrible trial to him to be so different and it is to his credit that he was able to adjust at all to the abnormal burden imposed upon him by a capricious nature.

Despite his problems, Edouard attempted to lead a normal life - which in the sheltered environment of Willow Bunch meant engaging in the horse and cattle business. Unfortunately, his curse of awkwardness attended him in this career and he suffered a bad fall from a horse which damaged his head and left his face noticeably distorted. As he grew older and his height increased, he had to abandon his dream of becoming a cowboy - *his feet dragged on the ground when he sat on a horse.*

By the time he was 17, Edouard stood 7 feet 1 inch

and was proportionately large in every other respect. A special bed had to be built for him, and all his clothing was tailor-made. Along with his bulk went the promise of incredible strength, and he once demonstrated this by lifting a horse weighing 800 pounds!

It was this promise of enormous strength that first launched him on his career as a strongman. News of his prowess reached beyond Willow Bunch to Moose Jaw, the natural trading magnet for the district, and from there to Montreal, the Canadian center for showmanship. Entrepreneur Eugene Tremblay invited the young man to Montreal to join his stable of noted strongmen, which then included Horace Barre and the imcomparable Louis Cyr.

Unknown to anyone during his sojourn in Montreal, Beaupre had contracted turberculosis and his enormous frame was already suffering from the ravages of the disease. While he was capable of short bursts of incredible strength, he lacked staying power, often spending a good deal of time resting. However, it was inevitable that - living in a stable of strongmen at Tremblay's - he would be involved in various feats. Newspaper men of the day promoted a wrestling match between him and Louis Cyr.

The bout took place in Sohmer Park on Monday, March 25, 1901, but it was no contest. Cyr, probably the strongest man of his day, was much quicker than his giant opponent, and literally ran circles around him. Edouard lacked the killer instinct and fell easy victim to the stronger, more aggressive Frenchman.

It was shortly after this that Edouard decided that the career of strongman was not his forte. He was, also, probably tiring of being the center of attraction whenever he left the gymnasium to stroll the streets of Montreal Crowds followed him everywhere, even intruding into cafes to watch him eat. He left Montreal in late 1901, and after a brief visit home, travelled to Montana to try again the life of a cowboy.

It was not to be, however, for he encountered all the old problems. In addition, he was still growing. Fortunately,

81

Edouard and friends, 1904 World's Fair

he acquired new friends - men who were not repelled by
his enormous height and size nor by his atrocious command
of the French and English languages. By pointing out to
him that he could never escape the curiosity of the crowds,
they persuaded him that his wisest course was to capitalize

on this fact and join a circus where his height and bulk would be an asset rather than a monstrous annoyance. In the end, he was convinced and signed up with an organizer named Davidson who was setting up acts for circuses and shows - among which was the forth-coming World's Fair to be held in St. Louis. M.

At the time of joining forces with Davidson, Edouard Beaupre stood 7 feet 11 inches and weighed nearly 370 pounds. His neck measured 21 inches and he could hold a foot ruler on the palm of his hand. His chest was nearly 57 inches.

To clothe such a giant frame privately would have been a financial disaster - especially since he kept outgrowing his clothing - but local St. Louis merchants came to the rescue, deeming it good advertising to supply his sartorial needs free of charge for the privilege of using his name and fame. Thus, the Willow Bunch Giant was always perfectly groomed.

As part of the publicity campaign for the World's Fair, the promoters hit upon the idea of a marriage between Edouard and Miss Ella Ewing, rated as the tallest woman in the world. She had been born near Goring, Missouri in either 1872 or 1875, and by the age of ten was reputed to have reached the height of 6 feet 9 inches. At the time of the proposed marriage, she was billed at 7 feet 6 inches.

Neither Miss Ewing nor Edouard were the slightest bit interested in the idea and the scheme was dropped. Miss Ewing lived to the age of 41, dying on January 10, 1913.

During his stint with the World's Fair in St. Louis, Edouard was one of the feature attractions of Fairyland. As part of his routine, he lifted heavy weights and performed other feats of strength. He was a great favorite with the crowds, especially the young people who viewed him as being the greatest human being they had ever seen. ¤ Beaupre's routine was more than an act, however, it was an increasingly difficult performance for him. After each stint on the platform, he had to retire in pain and exhaustion to his room where he collapsed on his huge cot.

83

Friends urged him to take a medical examination, but he
shrugged off their suggestions, saying that it was nothing
serious and would pass. Sometimes, his hacking cough
brought up flecks of blood.

But, it was serious, as the events of the night of
Saturday, July 2, 1904, revealed.

in the words of a friend, J.H. Noel, who was with
him that evening: "Towards 11:45, the show was finished.

84

At midnight, Beaupre, who was feeling tired, drank a cup of tea. Soon, he felt chest pains. he began to cough and bring up blood. he tried to undress himself to go to bed, but he could not. I advised him then to come to a doctor.

"He agreed, but then added in pain: 'I am going to die. It is sad to die so young and so far from dear parents.' He asked me for a glass of water. I ran in search of some, and on my return, Beaupre was already unconscious. The ambulance arrived and they took him to the Emergency Hospital where he died a few minutes later."

Edouard Beaupre's body was taken immediately to the morgue in St. louis. That evening, an autopsy was performed by Dr. R.B.H Granwohl and it is on the basis of his report that the Willow Bunch giant's claim to fame as the fourth tallest man in history is based. Dr. Granwohl recorded his height at 8' 3'' and his weight as 375.

He also remarked that while the bone structure was sound, the muscles were emaciated. It was incredible that Edouard could have daily performed feats of strength under such a handicap. The cause of death was tuberculosis of the lungs.

It is entirely possible that the gentle giant of Willow Bunch never received the dignity of a Christian burial. A strange series of events took place which renders this suspicion almost a certainty.....

Dr. J. maurice Blais, in his authoritative article in the **Canadian Medical Association Journal** for June, 1967, entitled simply *Edouard Beaupre, 1881-1904,* highlights some of the events. The body was removed from the morgue to the funeral parlors of Eberle and Keyes, at 1110 St. Ange for preparation to be taken back to Willow Bunch. There seemed to be an understanding that William Burke, manager of the World's Fair, would be responsible for the expenses. Whether this be true or not, the fact was that no expenses were forthcoming from that source. The shadowy figure of Mr. Davidson, who was reputedly Beaupre's manager, flitted about in the background of the confusion, but the man himself was of no help whatever to the undertakers. A telegram to Edouard's parents in Willow Bunch elicited the sad information that they had no funds to undertake the expense of bringing the giant home. The undertakers were confused and slightly angry. Since there was no money forthcoming, they decided to recoup their losses by displaying the body and charging admission to view it. They re-embalmed the corpse, bragging: "It should last on display for ten years," and exhibited it in a glass case in the window of a shop on the corner of Market and Broadway.

Disgusted by this example of bad taste, friends of the Beaupres contacted the North West Mounted Police in Moose Jaw. They, in turn, made representations to the St. Louis City Police, asking for an investigation. St. Louis responded by arresting the man Davidson and closing down the display.

However, Davidson was shortly released on bail - and it is doubtful that the charges were pursued any farther. What did happen was that the Willow Bunch giant was secretly moved to a new location in East St. Louis. He was again exhibited to the public, but in a much more discrete manner.

When information on the new exhibition reached the St. Louis police, they reacted swiftly by shutting down the show and issuing a stern warning to the promoters. Undaunted, the latter retaliated by moving the display again.

By some unknown method and secret manipulation, the body was smuggled across the border into Canada. It next turned up in the Eden Museum on St. Laurent Street close to the National Monument in Montreal. Here it was exhibited in the foyer for about six months.

Still, there was no record of a decent burial for the sad boy from Willow Bunch.

Instead, the greatest indignity of all was to be visited upon him. When the exhibition at the Eden Museum closed in the fall of 1906, the promoters disposed of the giant' body by unceremoniously dumping it in a shed in Bellerive Park.

There is some confusion about what happened next. One account, written by Ken Cukthbertson for the **Accent** in its July 12, 1980 issue, claims that the body was discovered by children playing in the park on November 18, 1906. The newspapers of the day, however, do not support this claim. Another account says that the corpse was not found until the spring of 1907. In any event, it is clear what transpired next.

The startling discovery was reported to the police, who called in a doctor from Maisonneuve. This man promptly identified the body as that of the famous Edouard Beaupre. This would have been the appropriate moment to accord the Willow Bunch giant his rightful due to a Christian burial even had his consecrated soil been a plot in Potter's Field. It was not to be, however, for the medical man called a colleague, Dr. Louis Napoleon Delorme, at the University of Montreal. The body was transported to the University by a drayman who charged them $25.00.

Once again the enormous cadaver was treated to a special embalming process and placed on display in a glass case in the anatomy department. From time to time it was removed for minute study by curious scientific men, but as time went on it became less of a curiosity and more of an embarassment. It was finally removed from public display in the 1970s and relegated to an obscure case in the basement.

It is a sad and tragic fact that over the years the real issue of Edouard Beaupre, the farm boy from Willow Bunch, Saskatchewan, has been overlooked. By a quirk of nature, he was denied a normal life and by the hand and avarice of man he has been denied the honor of resting peacefully in his native land. After all these years, he deserves to be returned to Willow Bunch for Christian burial and to be honored in his province. There is a lovely little museum in Willow Bunch, dedicated to his memory and it seems only fitting that he should be close at hand.

There has been some fear expressed by his living relatives that, should the body be brought home and buried at Willow Bunch, the grave might be vandalized and the remains spirited away. In this regard, it might be recalled that the same fear was expressed when another famous Westerner - Louis Riel - was buried at St. Boniface in late 1885. The problem was solved simply at that time by pouring a concrete mat over the site. Riel remains undisturbed to this date. Surely the fourth tallest man in history deserves the honor of return to his homeland!

Yip Luck - Highbinder

"I think I have located the Chinamen who went through James Whiteside's barn," Chief of Police Alexander Main announced to his wife on the morning of Saturday, April 14, 1900. "I am going out this morning to bring them in."

At 35, Chief Main was typical of most frontier police-men, tall, straight, muscular. He had arrived in British Columbia as a teenager and had signed on as a cannery worker. After rising through the ranks to a managerial position, he had accepted an offer to become Chief of Police for the fishing town of Steveston, B.C., on the western side of Lulu Island just south of Vancouver. His appoint-ment took place in 1898 and for two years he had carried out his job with apparent fairness and absolute fearless-ness. The bulk of his charges were Japanese and Chinese fishermen, though the white trade people and storekeepers also came under his jurdisdiction. His work brought him into close contact with members of the British Columbia Provincial Police and he had many friends on that force.

After breakfast, Chief Main left his home on the outskirts of Steveston and checked at his office and the jail before going to look for the Chinese men. He was accompanied by his dog.

Chief Main did not return home that evening as was his custom. When by Sunday morning he had still not showed up, Mrs Main became alarmed and went to the home of some friends to seek assistance.

A search party of local men was organized and visited all the local haunts of the popular Chief of Police. There was no trace of the missing man, but one resident told them that he had seen the Chief walking north from town with his dog. The posse concentrated its efforts in that direction.

About two miles from Steveston was a cabin containing seven Chinese fishermen. These told them that Chief Main had stopped by their place Saturday morning and after visiting had walked north in the direction of a cabin owned by Yip Luck, some 300 yards distance.

Yip Luck's cabin was located in the bush about a quarter mile back from the beach and roughly half way between the south and north arms of the Fraser River. A small space had been cleared around the cabin and a vegetable garden had been started to one side.

On arrival at Yip Luck's cabin, the search party found it occupied by three Chinese men. The owner, Yip Luck, was a dark complexioned man of 30, standing 5' 11'' and extremely well built and muscular. He had prominent, protruding front teeth. Those who knew him well believed that he was a highly-placed member of the notorious Highbinder secret tong.

The second man was Chanyee Chung, a small, self-effacing man who was very differential to those whom he considered his superiors. The third was a tall, slender Chinese named Kung Ah Wong who had arrived from china only a few weeks before and had been taken under Yip Luck's protection.

Since none of the posse spoke Chinese, conversation was difficult, but the searchers managed to convey the message that they were looking for Chief Alex Main. Chanyee Chung started to say something, but a fierce look from Yip Luck silenced him. It was Yip Luck who informed them in a wierd mixture of Pigin English and sign language that the Chief had passed their cabin the day before and continued on in a north-west direction towards the beach.

After leaving Yip Luck's cabin, the posse conferred and reached the tentative conclusion that there was something suspicious about the conduct of the three Chinese men. Yip Luck had been highly secretive and covertly hostile; but Chanyee Chung had been about to talk; while the third man had kept in the background but was obviously frightened about something. Nevertheless, their only lead was Luck's suggestion that the missing man had gone on. The search was continued through the rest of the day without a further clue to Chief Main's disappearance.

Returning to Steveston late that evening, the leaders of the posse decided to seek professional help and a message was sent to the B.C. Provincial Police in Vancouver.

Detective Wylie, a personal friend of Alexander Main, arrived from Vancouver Monday morning, accompanied by Constable Campbell. A new search party was formed which included a part bloodhound owned by the local blacksmith, George Shea. They went directly to the cabin of Yip Luck.

A thorough search of the cabin turned up a pipe and a pair of blue overalls which were identified as having been stolen from Whitehead's barn, but there was nothing that would tie Chief Main to the spot. Outside, there were several places in the sandy soil which revealed ashes, but this was not unusual for bush country.

The search was widened and extended towards the beach. Isiah Trites and his brother, Frank, noticed a patch of freshly turned earth about 100 yards from the cabin and the bloodhound was brought up. On sniffing the ground the dog became excited. Detective Wylie scraped away the loose soil and came upon clothing a few inches below the surface. Further digging revealed a circular grave and the body of Chief Alexander Main. His dog had been crammed in beside him. The grave had not been large enough to hold the policeman's large body and both his head and legs had been cut off in order to fit him inside.

It was then about three o'clock on the afternoon of Monday, April 17.

A farm wagon was brought and the Chief's body was removed to a temporary morgue in Steveston. The dog, whose head had also been severed, was left in its lonely grave.

After sending for Vancouver Coroner McQuigan to come to Steveston, Detective Wylie sat down with his colleague and discussed the meagre evidence they had amassed.

The only clue they had to go on was that seven Chinese fishermen had said that Main was seen walking in the direction of Yip Luck's cabin. He had evidently not been seen beyond that point. His grave was a scant hundred yards from Luck's shack. They decided that there was sufficient evidence pointing towards the three Chinamen to warrant bringing them in. It was also deemed wise to bring in the seven Chinese fisherman as material witnesses, since from their experience Orientals had a habit of disappearing when wanted for court.

Taking a Chinese interpreter named McLeod with them, Wylie and Campbell went first to the fishermen's shack and advised the occupants that they were to go straight to Steveston and tell what they knew about Chief Main. They then proceeded with some caution to Yip Luck's cabin. They found only Yip Luck and Chanyee Chuck. The third man had disappeared. Neither Luck nor Chanyee admitted knowing where their companion was.

Both men were arrested on suspicion of murder and taken back to Steveston to be housed in the local jail.

An attempt was made to question the taciturn Yip Luck, but he responded to all questions with indifference or no answer at all. He admitted that Chief Main had come to their shack on Saturday but had gone away north.

The diminutive Chanyee Chung, however, was much more talkative. He said that Chief Main had visited them Saturday and that as a result of an argument Yip Luck had killed him with a blow from a brush hook. In response to his story, Const. Campbell went to the cabin and came back with a long pole to which was attached a heavy curved knive used for scrubbing out underbrush. Chanyee identified this as the weapon with which the police officer had been murdered.

Nothing that the blade of the brush hook was partially rusted and patently had not been cleaned for a long time, the officers doubted that they had the right weapon. Chanyee also told them that the third man, Kung Ah Wong, had gone to the home of a cousin after the visit from the

search party on Sunday. The cousin had hid him. It was believed that he was now out of the country. On the strength of this, Kung's cousin was also arrested.

Coroner McQuigan arrived in Steveston about seven that evening and made immediate preparations for an inquest. Evidence was taken from the seven Chinese and they were released. Though Yip Luck and Chanyee were present, no attempt was made to question them.

The verdict, which found the three Chinese responsible for Alexander Main's death, was a foregone conclusion.

While the inquest was proceeding inside the old prison, a group of angry citizens gathered outside with the declared intention of lynching the three suspects. Among them were many Japanese fishermen, with whom Chief of Police Main had been a favorite. Just before midnight, Detective Wylie appeared at the prison door, informing them that the inquest was still in session and asking them to disperse. Silence greeted his request.

The truth was that the inquest was already over, but fearing the mood of the lynch mob, Wylie determined to keep them occupied at the front. He went directly from the front door and spirited the two prisoners out the back entrance. They were taken down a side street and put into a wagon that had been brought up for that purpose. While the mob waited for the inquest to conclude, the prisoners were hustled away to the sturdy provincial prison in New Westminister.

The would-be lynch mob did not learn of the deception until after midnight, but when they did they immediately transferred their wrath to the unfortunate man who had helped the third suspect to escape. Only a strong plea from the jailor and police prevented them from attacking the old structure. Reluctantly, they dispersed and returned to their homes in the early morning darkness.

With Yip Luck and Chanyee Chung safely in the provincial prison, Detective Wylie and his men turned their attention to the third member of the gang. At the same time, the Chinese Board of Trade in Vancouver, expressing horror at the murder, began raising a fund to hire Chinese detectives to track down the fugitive.

Re-questioning the man who had assisted Kung Ah Wong, Wylie learned from him that the fugitive had come to his home on Sunday evening and had told him what had happened. Since Kung Ah Wong professed that he had taken no part in the murder, the cousin had sheltered him Sunday night and late the next night had sent him to other friends who had hidden him in Steveston. On Thursday, April 19, his friends had rowed the wanted man across the river to Ladner and had passed him to compatriots who had promised to help him escape into the United States. Their actions had been just in time, for on Thursday night, angry townspeople had raided the Chinese Quarter of Steveston searching for the suspect.

Wylie did not learn of this until early Friday morning and suspected that he might already be too late. Nevertheless, he went directly to Ladner with a Chinese interpreter. From one source, he learned that Kung Ah Wong had been sheltered there the previous night and that he had been given directions to what was known locally as the Semiahmoo Trail. This was an underground railway leading from Ladner to the United States and had been used in the past to smuggle Chinese people into Washington state. It was assumed that Kung Ah Wong was even then speeding southward along this smuggler's highway.

Though the fugitive had several hours headstart, Wylie secured the services of a local Chinese guide and started along the Semiahmoo Trail. To his suprise, after covering only a few miles of the serpentine path, they saw their quarry coming towards them. Kuong Ah Wong had become thoroughly confused in his directions, turned around and believed that he was heading south when he was actually returning north!

The tall Chinaman made no resistance when taken into custody. Indeed, Wylie got the impression that he was quite relieved that his flight was over. On the trip back to New Westminster, he made a full confession. Speaking through an interpreter, he told Wylie that Chief Main had come to their cabin on Saturday morning and found Yip Luck and Chanyee Chung on the beach. (This was later confirmed by a Captain Atkinson whose boat was passing along the shore at the time and who had seen Chief Main and the two Chinese men talking on the beach.) Chief of Police Main had then come to the cabin, and noticing some stolen tools lying on the floor, had taken out a notebook and began to make a list.

While he was thus engaged, Yip Luck slipped out of the cabin and returned moments later carrying a two-bitted axe. As Main was bending over in one corner to take a closer look at some items, Yip came up behind him and dealt him a murderous blow with the axe. To make sure that his victim was dead, Yip had then cut his throat with a heavy knife.

Covering the body with a blanket, the three men had gone out into the garden and worked through the rest of the forenoon as if nothing unusual had taken place. After dinner, they returned inside and killed a chicken. They spread the blood over the floor to ward off any evil spirits.

Later, with nightfall, Chanyee had dug a grave, but it proved to be too small. They had cut off the man's head and legs to make the body fit the hole. There were several patches of blood both inside and outside the cabin and these they covered by burning wood to cover the stains with ashes.

Kung Ah Wong said that both he and Chanyee Chung were afraid of Yip Luck. He had told them that he had killed other white men and that if they told anyone what had happened he would turn them over to the Highbinders. Nevertheless, after the search party had visited the cabin on Sunday, he had decided to seek the assistance of his cousin. Friends had hidden him out in Steveston until

Thursday, when they took him across the river to friends in Ladner.

Certain now that the police had a case, Detective Wylie had the three men charged with murder. However, Kung Ah Wong was never to stand trial for his life. Shortly after entering prison, it was found that he was suffering from an advanced case of tuberculosis. He died before coming to trial.

The Fall Assize openes on Tuesday, October 2, 1900, before Mr. Justice Irving. The Crown, represented by Mr. Bowser, planned to try Yip Luck first, as it planned to rely heavily upon Chung as Queen's Witness.

Though Yip Luck was unrepresented by counsel, the Crown anticipated a difficult trial, for he was known to be highly intelligent and cunning. To the surprise of everyone, Yip Luck startled the court by announcing that he was guilty. "Yes, I killed him. That all I got to say."

His plea of guilty was accepted and he was returned to his cell so that the trial of Chanyee might proceed.

In view of the fact that Yip Luck has assumed all the blame for the murder - plus the fact that it was his story that first led the police to fasten the guilt - Chanyee Chung was quickly arraigned and pleaded not guilty. His plea was likewise accepted at face value and he was acquitted without trial. He walked from the court a free, though frightened little man.

Brought before his Honor, Mr. Irving that afternoon for sentencing, the usually taciturn Yip Luck was very voluble when asked if he had anything to say before sentence was passed. Speaking through Interpretor Cumyow, Yip Luck stated that all three men had been involved in a series of thefts in British Columbia and the state of Washington to the south. He accused Chief Alex Main of extorting tribute from many Chinese of the Highbinder tong, of which he was leader. He had also tried to force Yip Luck and his friends to cut wood for him at a ridiculously low figure. It had been determined by the Highbinders that Main should die for his treatment of them.

On the day of the murder, Chief Main had come to his cabin, accusing him of possessing stolen tools. The three of them had killed him with an axe. He and Kung Ah Wong, whom he called 'Sam'', had carried the Chief's body to the makeshift grave. The dog had been killed by Kung Ah Wong, while held by Yip Luck.

After disposing of the body, Kung Ah Wong had kept the policeman's revolver for himself, but they had thrown all the other stuff in the ocean.

Mr. Justice Irving, distresssed by Yip Luck's accusation that Chief Main had carried on an extortion racket, was visibly disturbed as he sentenced the dark-faced Chinese man to be hanged on November 16. A reporter remarked that Yip Luck had heard the sentence translated without a tremor and "walked from the courtroom with the same dogged firmness that has always characterized his behaviour.''

Yip Luck accepted his fate with a calm that was chilling to his jailors. He spent part of his time in the death cell carving a tombstone for his grave. On it he inscribed his name, age, birthdate and the final notation that he had been executed November 16, 1900. When it was done, he turned it over with sufficient money to the authorities to ship both it and his body back to China.

He was visited daily by a Chinese missionary, Thomas Touche, and at his urging made a "clean sweep'' of his crimes. He detailed a series of robberies carried out in both Canada and the United States, some of which he participated in and others which were carried out by members of the Highbinder tong under his direction. He also revealed that he had killed two men in the state of Washington.

On contacting authorities in Washington, the police learned that his accounts of these slayings tallied exactly with the information on file with the local sheriffs.

When he was brought from his cell on the morning of November 16, Sheriffs Zimmerman and Eastabrook, of Washington, were on hand to witness his execution. The hanging was carried out in the courtyard of the provincial prison at New Westminster. The hangman, Radcliffe, had taken a shot of whiskey too many before being called upon to perform his deadly art and did not notice that the trap was not functioning smoothly. Recent rains had swollen the trap so that it required three tries before it swung loose. Yip Luck faced this, as he had other events in his life, with quiet fatalism. He died with all the dignity that could be mustered under the terrible circumstances.

We wish to acknowledge the kind assistance of Mr. Ovila Lesperance, of Willow Bunch, Saskatchewan, nephew of the famed Edouard Beaupre, in the preparation of the story on the Willow Bunch Giant.

PHOTO CREDITS

Glenbow Foundation, Calgary: pp. 7, 11, 14, 64, 67, 74 and 75.
Manitoba Archives: pp. 18, 20, 22
Ovila Lesperance: pp. 78, 82.
The Province, Vancouver, 48, 51, 54, 57 and 58.
B.C. Archives: pp 30 and 32
Frontier Collection: page 56

STAFF ARTISTS: Blanche McLeod and Sandra Santa Lucia